MW00608206

Go Tax Free

Go Tax Free

17 Ways to Grow and Protect Your Wealth
and Choose How You Want to Be Taxed

By Karl F. Frank CFP®, MBA, MSF

Copyright © 2013 by Karl Frank.

ISBN: 978-0-9889197-0-9

Library of Congress Catalog Card Number: 2013904807

All rights reserved. No part of this book may be reproduced or transmitted in any form or by any means, electronic or otherwise, including photocopying, recording or by information storage and retrieval systems, without the written permission of the author, except by a reviewer who may quote brief passages in a review.

Limit of Liability/Disclaimer of Warranty. While the author and publisher have used their best efforts in preparing this book, they make no representations or warranties with respect to the accuracy or completeness of the contents of this book and specifically disclaim any implied warranties of merchantability or fitness for a particular purpose. No warranty may be created or extended by sales representatives or written sales materials. The advice and strategies contained herein may not be suitable for your situation. You should consult with a professional where appropriate. Neither the publisher nor author shall be liable for any loss of profit or any other commercial damages, including but not limited to special, incidental, consequential, or other damages.

Printed in the United States of America.

Table of Contents

Acknowledgements

I'd like to thank my wife and lifetime guide, Stacey, for all her support and for keeping me on the right path.

Thank you to our team and to Cameron Morgan, Judson Cass, Chad Harmon, and Mike Miller, who served as subject-matter experts.

Art and Inge Rewinkel, your influence is omnipresent in this book.

Kristin Sesko, whose confidence and can-do spirit is infectious.

Debra Fine, you got Stacey and I unstuck at a critical point, and your success shows the way.

Thanks to our clients for living these plans and inspiring the book.

Thanks to Morgan and Henry Frank and my family for your motivation and love!

Thanks to God for bringing a little snow to the ski slopes.

Foreword

The information provided in this book is for general purposes only and is subject to change without notice. Every effort has been made to compile this material from reliable sources; however, no warranty can be made as to its accuracy or completeness. The information presented does not represent, warranty, or imply that any strategies or methods of analysis offered will be successful or that they can or will predict future results or insulate investors from losses. Investing involves risk, including the potential loss of principal. Past performance is not a guarantee of future results.

With the exception of my personal stories, the characters and examples in this work are fictitious. Any resemblance to real persons, living or dead, is purely coincidental.

At the time of printing, all tax information was current according to IRS rules as of January 1, 2013. The information is not intended to be tax or legal advice and it may not be relied on for the purpose of avoiding tax liabilities and tax penalties. It is important to note that tax legislation and tax rules are constantly changing, and the reader is strongly encouraged to seek tax and legal advice from qualified, professional advisors regarding their own personal financial circumstances.

Introduction

Absolute: We pay more in taxes than we do in food, shelter and clothing combined. —Tax Foundation[i]

Why This Book?

My father just quit. He left the mountain town of Evergreen, Colorado, drove down to Denver and purchased a quarter-million dollar, depreciating retirement plan on eight wheels.

Then he paused. A 40 foot, Class A mobile home wasn't big enough for Tom Frank. So he bought two mopeds and put them on the front. He bought a satellite dish for the roof and a Suzuki four-by-four for a trailer. What he did next may not be legal in many states, but my father was an attorney. Anyone who has worked with a powerful attorney knows that laws are just written opinions and only his opinion matters. So my dad purchased a boat to tow behind the four-by-four. My parents had more axles in their retirement dream than cars have wheels.

Thus outfitted, my mother and father set off on their retirement journey together. Six months into their retirement they made it to the Baja peninsula in Mexico. My father fell sick with a chest cold. Thank the Lord my mother was a farm girl and could drive anything, so she turned around the Frank Family Train and headed back to Colorado, slowly. It took about 10 days.

By the time they arrived in Evergreen, our family doctor said, "Tom, you need a biopsy. This is more than a chest cold." We checked him into Lutheran Hospital on Friday and he died on Sunday. Mesothelioma: a fast-acting, painful form of lung cancer commonly associated with asbestos.

My father had a six-month retirement.

What happened next changed the course of my life.

My father was a business owner. He did not plan to leave the business. He just left. My mother became a business owner. It wasn't fair to the other folks in the business; they lost their rain maker. It wasn't fair to my mother who had no right (or desire) to be in business. The other attorneys scattered after my father passed away. My mother received a fraction of the business' value before my father's passing. But that small amount may have been appropriate. After all, what is a business worth without a rain maker?

My mother has a good financial advisor. She will never be destitute, but her greatest asset today is time, not money, and she has less than she would like.

I cannot help enough small business owners avoid what happened to my father. This passion drives every decision we make at our firm. Every difficult decision I face brings me back to the moment Dad just quit. As I contemplate what advice to give, I ask myself this question: What would I do if you were my father?

How to Use This Book

Go Tax Free is full of ideas to help you on your unique journey. You will finish this book with a basic knowledge of tax and investment strategies that are both powerful and practical. You will be able to talk to professionals effectively and know how to avoid many expensive mistakes.

The first two chapters cover the absolute truths about tax-deferred and tax-free financial plans. Each subsequent chapter summarizes a handful of good ideas with examples of their applications and their shortcomings. Some ideas are ways to earn tax deductions today. Some ideas defer taxes into the future. Some ideas accumulate money in a manner that is never taxed again.

Every idea is not for everyone. In fact, many of these ideas will not work for your situation. However, you may be presented with one or more of these ideas on your investing journey by one or more investment professionals. Basic knowledge of these ideas will help you avoid wasting time and money.

Optionally, read the Appendices to skip to the chapters that may make the most sense for you. You may be employed or not employed. You may be more concerned with safety or more concerned with growth. You may have a long time horizon or a short one.

Use this book. Make notes in it. Ask questions. Bring it to your meetings with your advisors. Ask them if an idea presented here may be useful for you. Get engaged! Learn to love the process of planning your money.

A Natural and Mandatory Relationship

You and your money have a relationship. It is natural. It is mandatory. It is good.

Alone, you have no need for money. Money exists only because of relationships. You learn much about your relationships with others by looking at where money is spent and why.

You become clearer about your identity when you look at where you actually spend your money. With greater knowledge, you can clarify your intentions. The more clear your intentions, the less important the distractions that separate you from your wealth and your true identity. The more money you have, the more resources you have to achieve what is most important to you.

Your money relationship is natural and mandatory and good. By pursuing wealth, you are pursuing your true self. Money can be an expression of love. As evidence, I present to you your checkbook. Look at where you spend your money. Is it spent on people and on activities of importance?

It is natural and healthy to want more resources. Money enables us to spend time with people we love, doing activities that are pleasing to us, in places where we love to be.

Your money relationship is mandatory. A very wise CEO once told me, "Nothing worth doing is easy." She made a living being the first at everything. Whether you are an accomplished investor or this is your first step toward that end, you must take charge of your money to take charge of your life. Money and happiness can be symbiotic and harmonious. Even if thinking about money gives you fits, then consider this: The more you learn, the less stressful it becomes.

Do you feel concerned that you should have more money? Have you ever felt guilty about wanting more (because so many people have so much less)?

Or are you concerned, after having accumulated what you have, that you could be swindled? You don't know enough? You don't have anyone to trust?

It is time to recognize that these emotions drive your decisions. It is time to address your money relationship.

Amateur Hour is Over

When we are honest with ourselves, we know that we can change our own course. We also know that we must, individually and collectively, make a change to achieve our intentions. If we do nothing actively, merely aging in a changing world will change our course for us.

Amateur hour is over. The immeasurable obligations and unfunded liabilities of the United States cannot be overstated. Our annual budget deficit is $1 trillion[ii]. In a different time, with a different worldview, this would mean something big. Today, we have lost our perspective on big.

Imagine this. I ask you to walk into my office. Sit in this comfortable chair. Show me a wheelbarrow full of your life savings. For convenience sake, we'll call it one million dollars.

Congratulations, that is roughly $1 million more than the average American has saved!

Thank you for all of your money, I say. I give it to Uncle Sam. You are now broke.

I repeat this with 100 families just like you. One hundred other advisors repeat this process with 100 of their clients. Just like you, each of them accumulated $1 million. This is 10,000 former millionaires now bankrupt. But this is not enough. One trillion dollars is the life savings of one million millionaires.

Every year, the federal government outspends itself at a rate that would bankrupt one million millionaires.

What's worse, until recently, it was twice that rate every year.

Now more than ever, we must prepare our own future and not depend upon the kindness of strangers. The good news is that we can.

A Toolbox and Not a Hammer

Many of the best financial planning ideas turn into poorly delivered sales pitches by well-intentioned amateurs. Either the sales representatives are A) too deep in their product to see other options or B) too well (or too poorly) compensated to grab another hammer. Every problem they face becomes a nail to pound with only one tool.

This book is a toolbox, not a hammer. Use it as a reference, a starting point for a conversation with your experts. Go forward with confidence that anything you do not know, you can learn. And anything that is still incomprehensible, after you've given it your best shot, is not right for you and you should move on and look elsewhere.

Another path awaits you, just around the bend.

Poor writing (about life insurance in particular) is one of the most egregious problems in the money industry. Books that espouse one plan dismiss almost every other plan as inferior, irrelevant, or prone to government interference.

Absolute: Every plan is prone to (government or other) interference.

We must live symbiotically with government and large corporations just as we live with neighbors. The more we know, the better we coexist.

Plans are worthless without action. Actions are priceless.

It's been said that the poor man has a million plans and they all start tomorrow. Unlike him, you must take action to be successful. The sailboat must move before the rudder can steer. This book will help you steer in your intended direction. By the conclusion of this book, you will know many of the most important benefits and limitations of tax-saving navigational tools. You will then be able to move with the confidence that you can "take a sounding," changing course if and when you choose.

Choosing Professional Help

Almost every idea in this book requires the help of a professional to put into motion. Professionals will not work for free, but they will tell you how much they are paid and by whom. They will tell you the limits of their abilities and their knowledge. They will do what they do best.

Professionals do not work alone. They work with a team of other professionals who complement and compensate for their skills and the necessary limits under the law. No one has the answers to everything except the amateur, and the IRS eats amateurs for lunch.

You will have enough knowledge to feel like an amateur by the end of this book. Your great strength will be that you can identify other amateurs. Avoid them at all costs. Instead, look for professionals.

What Professionals Ask of You

Professionals ask questions, a lot of questions, before they provide advice. What is appropriate for your coworker, your relative, or your wealthy neighbor is not appropriate for you. This is not a "maybe." It is an absolute.

What is appropriate for someone else is not appropriate for me.

Professionals know this. The hammer may be one person's solution, but it is everyone else's problem. The hammer is not what you deserve, but it is what you may have come to expect. Learn to expect more.

The Internet profoundly worsens your plight. Information is not knowledge. A Google of information is not ingenious. It is noise. The professional you want to work with, and need to find, is one who translates the noise into your unique tune.

Ask yourself, "What does my professional advisor know about:"

- My values?
- My goals?
- The people who are most important to me?
- My other assets not under his or her management?
- My other professional advisors?
- The process that I want to follow, not necessarily what is convenient for him or her?
- My interests outside of money?

An excellent financial professional implements a discovery process safely, without a hidden agenda. You are on a unique voyage and your guide had better know what sights you want to see along the way and what sights you do not. If your financial guide does not know the answers to these questions, then how can he or she help you on the journey? Move on.

The Characteristics Professionals Share

Think about the professionals you know.

Doctors are confident, knowledgeable, and limited in scope. They follow a strict code of ethics.

Attorneys share all of the above characteristics. Most professional attorneys are specialists. They follow a strict code of ethics.

Certified Public Accountants (CPAs) are focused on areas of expertise. Not all of them are tax experts and they will tell you so. In fact, many tax experts are Enrolled Agents and may or may not be CPAs. They all follow a strict code of ethics.

Professionals work for the long-term. They put their clients' interests ahead of their own. They make the complex simple. They help clients avoid big mistakes.

Professional financial planners follow a similar path. While not universal, the best financial planners swear a fiduciary oath to put the financial interests of their clients ahead of their own. Certified Financial Planner® (CFP), among other marks, denotes professionalization within the financial services industry. As a start, look for that mark in your search for professional financial help.

Questions to Ask a Professional

Here is a list of questions to ask a professional. Many of the best professionals answer these questions on their websites. You do not even need an interview before they have passed (or failed) your first screen test.

After visiting the financial planner's website, bring your unanswered questions to the first meeting and ask them. Do your homework. This gives you even greater confidence that you will find the best professional for your unique situation.

Pre-Interview Questions

Here are useful pre-interview questions:[iii]

- How long have you provided financial planning services?
- In what area(s) of financial planning do you specialize, if any?
- Do you have any advanced degrees, certificates or financial planning credentials?
- What securities and insurance licenses do you hold?

- How often have you performed similar services in the past?
- What type of financial planning services do you think I need based on my goals?
- On average, how long have your financial planning clients used your services?
- What independent organizations may I contact to verify your credentials, such as the Financial Industry Regulatory Authority (FINRA), the Securities and Exchange Commission (SEC), and the Financial Planning Association (FPA)?
- How are you compensated for your services?
- Which companies will custody my accounts and what are their financial situations?

Plus, ask questions of your own.

After the Interview

After your initial interview with the financial planner, ask yourself:

- Does this person have a process that makes it safe for me?
- Does he or she routinely work with folks like me?
- Will I learn from him or her and enjoy this journey?

Then conduct the due diligence, follow up on your promises, and move ahead.

In Our End is Our Beginning

I will end this chapter where I began, with a true story.

Art and Inge built a nice lifestyle by building their own business. Classic entrepreneurs, they owned more than one company before they founded A & I Financial Services LLC. They intended this company to be their last.

Art was a life insurance and investment professional. Inge was a top-notch tax preparer. Together, they raised two beautiful daughters, put them through college, and watched them marry and raise children of their own.

Along the way, one of their son-in-laws faced a series of family tragedies, including his father's death. This struck the young man quite hard. Art picked up the young man, brought him into the business and taught him how to walk, talk, live, and breathe the life of a professional.

Art said, "Just one hour a day. If you spend only one hour a day learning something new about your profession, you will succeed."

I did what I was told.

In 2009, my wife and I sent Art and Inge sailing on their retirement dreams when we completed a multi-year buy-out of A & I Financial Services LLC. Their last good idea is realized in the hard work our team does for a small number of successful families.

I am positive that you found this book for good reason and that you will achieve what you intend.

From my father's tragedy to my in-laws' success, I live the dreams of business owners. Our team eats and breathes the same advice we give.

By the time you reach the conclusion of this book and read the best story I know, you will know the next step you need to take to realize your dream.

Take that step.

Go Tax Deferred in an IRA

Absolute: "Anyone may so arrange his affairs that his taxes shall be as low as possible; he is not bound to choose that pattern which will best pay the Treasury; there is not even a patriotic duty to increase one's taxes." — Gregory v. Helvering, 69 F.2d 809, 810 (2d Cir. 1934), Judge Learned Hand

How This Benefits Me

Learn the rules around IRAs and the absolute features of tax-deferral, both the good and bad. Make wise financial decisions.

Example

Dempsey defers as much money into his IRA every year as he is allowed by law. During his working career, he has worked for six different companies and, each time upon exiting, has rolled his 401k into a tax-deferred IRA. Because of this, he has kept himself in a lower tax bracket over all these years than he would have been otherwise. Plus, he has money to spend when he changes from full-time work to full-time fun sometime in the next few years.

Overview

Before we begin, we need to understand taxes. We need to understand marginal taxes, long-term capital gains, and the Social Security provisional income tax (often an unpleasant surprise for retirees). We will look at the similarities between many tax-deferred investment vehicles. We will cover the fundamentals of IRAs, including contributions, rollovers, and required minimum distributions. We will look at an example of how taxation affects our investments over time, and at the pros and cons of investing money this way.

Income Tax

In 1913, Congress created the federal income tax as a way to fund the war. Many of us today can hardly imagine a federal government not receiving the income tax—or a worker earning money without paying it. However, 1913 was not that long ago. Would you like to return to a world without an income tax? Why not?

Let's look at the way income tax is structured today. Most of us think of our taxes as effective taxes, or the average amount of money we pay out of our gross salary, which is right around 20% for a large number of Americans. In fact, the federal government uses a graduated tax system of tax brackets. This progressive system taxes people who make less money at lower tax rates. The following chart summarizes the federal income tax system after the passage of the American Taxpayer Relief Act of 2012.[iv]

Federal Income Tax Brackets For Unmarried Individuals, Year 2013

(Other than Surviving Spouses and Heads of Households)

Lower $	Higher $	Tax %
$1	$8,925	10%
$8,926	$36,250	15%
$36,251	$87,850	25%
$87,851	$183,250	28%
$183,251	$398,350	33%
$398,351	$400,000	35%
$400,001	$999,999	39.6%

Federal Income Tax Brackets For Married Filing Joint, Year 2013

Lower $	Higher $	Tax %
$1	$17,850	10%
$17,851	$72,500	15%
$72,501	$146,400	25%
$146,401	$223,050	28%
$223,051	$398,350	33%
$398,351	$450,000	35%
$450,001	$999,999	39.6%

The first money you earn in a year is taxed at 10%. Every dollar you earn from there to the next level is taxed at 15%. From there to the next threshold, every dollar is taxed at 25%, and so on.

Add an additional percentage for a state income tax. For residents of Colorado, we pay a 4.63% state income tax. So if you're in the 10% federal tax bracket, you're really paying more than 14% when you count the state income tax. It's the same for every bracket. Some states have no income tax, other states are similar to Colorado, and, in many cities, residents also pay local income taxes.[v]

Most financial planners use the marginal tax bracket. Why is that?

When a financial planner looks at your taxes, he or she makes deductions from the top of your income. For example, a family with a $165,000 combined income may have an annual deductible mortgage interest payment that totals $15,000. They are in the 28 percent federal bracket, plus state tax. Mortgage interest payments are deductible, so their taxable income is reduced by $15,000. This means their taxable income is $150,000, which is in the 28 plus 4.63 percent tax bracket. They will be taxed at approximately 33%. If they hadn't made that $15,000 payment, they would have paid taxes at the *marginal rate* on that $15,000 of income. By making that interest payment, they save paying 33% of $15,000 to federal and state governments. This is a savings of $4,894.50.

If the family above were making payments into a tax-qualified plan, it's the same concept. Taxable income includes a deduction for a payment into a tax-deferred plan.

Long-Term Capital Gains Tax

The second primary way that investments are taxed is through the long-term capital gains tax. (Long-term means that the investment is held for more than a year.) Long-term capital gains are taxed at the following rates in 2013:[vi]

Long-Term Capital Gains Tax Rates, Year 2013

Single	Married Filing Joint	
$0 to $35,350	$0 to $70,700	0%
$35,350 to $400,000	$70,700 to $450,000	15%
$400,000 or more	$450,001 or more	20%

We will see in the following pages an example of how an investment taxed at the long-term capital gains rate compares with an investment that is taxed at the marginal tax rate. Clearly, the lower the tax rate, the more investment dollars the investor is able to keep. This is the appeal of tax-deferred investing plans.

Social Security Provisional Income Tax

For many Americans, Social Security income is taxed in retirement. At the end of the year, many retirees send money back to the IRS that Social Security sent them during that year. It sounds crazy and awful, and it is both of these things.

The Social Security system is designed to care for the folks who cannot care for themselves. The Social Security provisional income tax does not reward savers. Income from IRAs and other tax-deferred retirement vehicles are included in a new tax grid. The greater your retirement income, the lower your Social Security income will be. It does not matter how much you contributed to Social Security while you were working. Savers do not receive the same benefits as those who did not (and perhaps could not) save for retirement.

Here is how the Social Security provisional income tax works. Add half your Social Security benefit and all of your other taxable income to calculate your provisional income.

Social Security provisional income tax

1/2 Social Security Benefit/Year	
All Other Taxable Income	+
Provisional Income	=

Take your provisional income and compare it to one of the following charts depending on whether you are Single or Married Filing Joint or a Surviving Spouse (MFJOSS).[vii]

Provisional Income Tax Brackets For Social Security, Year 2013

	Single	M.F.J.O.S.S.
85% Taxable	> $35,000	> $44,000
50% Taxable	$25,001 to $34,999	$32,001 to $33,999
No Additional Taxes	< $25,000	< $32,000

The Social Security provisional income tax makes up to 85% of a person's Social Security retirement income subject to the same marginal income tax rate as the rest of their income.

Important: Income from tax-deferred plans is included in provisional income.

Distributions (income) from tax-deferred accounts, like IRAs and 401ks, are included in the provisional income tax calculation. Distributions from Roth IRAs and other tax-free accounts are not. We will look at this in more detail later.

Tax-Deferred Plans

Tax-deferred retirement plans come in many shapes and sizes, including:

- 401k, 403b, 457
- IRA, SEP IRA, SIMPLE, KEOGH
- Qualified plan: A tax-deductible, tax-deferred investment plan that qualifies with IRS rules.

All tax-deferred plans share the following features:

- Tax-deductible funding
- Tax-deferred growth
- Taxed at marginal income tax rates **upon withdrawal**
- Subject to estate taxes upon death and then marginal income tax rates of beneficiaries after that

There is no way to pull money out of a qualified plan like a traditional IRA without paying the marginal income tax rate.

One way to think about a qualified plan is this: You invest $10,000. Uncle Sam invests $5,000. Your tax-deferred plan has $15,000 at the beginning of the investment year. However, Uncle Sam is your proportional silent partner in this investment. Upon withdrawal, the federal government requires you to pay it back its proportional amount of the investment—your marginal income tax rates at that point in time. If the investment has grown to $150,000, you might owe $50,000.

IRA Fundamentals

The tax-deferred IRA is the final resting spot for most, if not all, of the other qualified tax-deferred investment vehicles. The IRA can be funded with contributions or rollovers.

IRA Contribution Limits for 2013

In 2013, the contribution limits are the smaller of:

- $5,500, or $6,500 if you're age 50 or older or
- Your earned income for the year

Both a husband and wife may make contributions for the calendar year. A non-working spouse may contribute up to the same amount.

Tax Deductions for 2013

If neither you nor your spouse is covered by a retirement plan at work, then 100% of your contribution is a tax deduction, regardless of your income.

If you are offered a retirement plan at work, then the deductibility of your IRA contribution is phased out depending upon your income.[viii]

Offered a Plan at Work

If Your Filing Status Is...	And Your Modified AGI Is...	Then You Can Take...
single or head of household	$59,000 or less	a full deduction up to the amount of your contribution limit.
	more than $59,000 but less than $69,000	a partial deduction.
	$69,000 or more	no deduction.
married filing jointly or qualifying widow(er)	$95,000 or less	a full deduction up to the amount of your contribution limit.
	more than $95,000 but less than $115,000	a partial deduction.
	$115,000 or more	no deduction.
married filing separately	less than $10,000	a partial deduction.
	$10,000 or more	no deduction.

If you file separately and did not live with your spouse at any time during the year, your IRA deduction is determined under the "Single" filing status.

If you are not covered by a plan at work, you can deduct contributions as long as your income falls within the following limits:[ix]

Not Offered a Plan at Work

If Your Filing Status Is...	And Your Modified AGI Is...	Then You Can Take...
single, head of household, or qualifying widow(er)	any amount	a full deduction up to the amount of your contribution limit.
married filing jointly or separately with a spouse who is not offered a plan at work	any amount	a full deduction up to the amount of your contribution limit.
married filing jointly with a spouse who is offered a plan at work	$178,000 or less	a full deduction up to the amount of your contribution limit.
	more than $178,000 but less than $188,000	a partial deduction.
	$188,000 or more	no deduction.
married filing separately with a spouse who is offered a plan at work	less than $10,000	a partial deduction.
	$10,000 or more	no deduction.

If you file separately and did not live with your spouse at any time during the year, your IRA deduction is determined under the "Single" filing status.

Age Limits

After age 70½, you can no longer contribute to your traditional IRA. Instead, you have to make required minimum distributions, or RMDs, which will be discussed in short order.

Rollovers

The contribution limits do not include rollovers from other qualified tax-deferred investment vehicles, like a 401k. You can rollover your money from another qualified tax-deferred vehicle in one of two ways.

A direct rollover transfers the money institution to institution, and incurs no tax penalty. You never touch the money during this transfer. It is usually the preferred method.

An indirect rollover transfers the money to you, in your name. You then deposit the money and write a check to the new institution. The indirect rollover must be completed within 60 days or the transfer becomes taxable.

Required Minimum Distributions

Qualified tax-deferred plans force the owners and beneficiaries to pull out money according to the IRS schedules whether or not the person wants or needs the money. This is complicated and unfortunate. As we age, the last thing we want to worry about is stumbling over another IRS guideline, especially this one. If we make a mistake, the penalty is 50% of the required distribution. Ouch! So let's make sure we really understand how the RMDs work.

RMDs begin April 1st the year following the owner's age of 70½. This date is called the Required Beginning Date (RBD). Failure to receive the RMD by the RBD triggers a 50% excise tax on the undistributed amount.

IRS Publication 590 includes three tables used to determine the amount of the RMD:

Table 1 – Single Life Expectancy for Use by Beneficiaries

Table 2 – Joint Life and Last Survivor Expectancy for use by owners whose spouses are more than 10 years younger and are the sole beneficiaries of the IRA

Table 3 – Uniform Lifetime for use by Unmarried Owners, by Married Owners whose spouses are not more than 10 years younger, and Married Owners whose spouses are not the sole beneficiary of their IRA.

Most people use Table 3, below. To calculate the RMD, divide the value of the traditional IRA on December 31st of the prior year by the divisor from the applicable table.[x]

IRS Uniform Lifetime Table 3

Age	RMD Divisor	Age	RMD Divisor	Age	RMD Divisor
70	27.4	86	14.1	102	5.5
71	26.5	87	13.4	103	5.2
72	25.6	88	12.7	104	4.9
73	24.7	89	12.0	105	4.5
74	23.8	90	11.4	106	4.2
75	22.9	91	10.8	107	3.9
76	22.0	92	10.2	108	3.7
77	21.2	93	9.6	109	3.4
78	20.3	94	9.1	110	3.1
79	19.5	95	8.6	111	2.9
80	18.7	96	8.1	112	2.6
81	17.9	97	7.6	113	2.4
82	17.1	98	7.1	114	2.1
83	16.3	99	6.7	115	1.9
84	15.5	100	6.3		
85	14.8	101	5.9		

The RMD can have a significantly negative impact upon a person's retirement. We investigate this unfortunate situation next.

Bob and Joyce

An example will help to illustrate the RMD effects. Let's say Joyce and Bob both turned 70½ in the prior year and now they must take RMDs. Joyce has one IRA worth $1 million and Bob has five IRAs that total $1 million. Joyce has to withdraw $36,496 this year. Bob has to either take five separate RMDs, one from each account, totaling $36,496, or take one large withdrawal from one account.

RMD for Bob or Joyce

IRA Amount	$ 1,000,000
RMD Divisor	27.4
RMD	$ 36,496

Next year, they will each take the sum of their accounts and divide by the age 71 divisor, 26.5. The divisor shrinks every year. The amount they must withdraw, as a percentage of the whole, increases every year.

The required minimum distributions are a lot to track, especially when a person has a lot of small accounts. For these reasons, I often recommend that investors consolidate the number of accounts they hold in retirement. Remember, having multiple accounts should not be confused with diversification. Little to nothing is to be gained by holding a large number of small IRAs.

Some people make the mistake of thinking that holding more than one IRA or 401k is diversification. Investments are not well diversified by holding a large number of small accounts. Instead, diversification means holding a good variety of uncorrelated investments.

Some experts claim that each IRA should have a beneficiary and that holding more than one IRA, or even splitting IRAs into separate, small accounts, is advantageous over the long haul. There are few, if any, risks more costly than the 50% penalty imposed by missing an RMD payment. When choosing the number of IRAs for your situation, I recommend keeping things as simple as possible.

Comparing a Tax-Deferred Account to a Taxable Account

A tax-deferred account avoids paying taxes upon the initial investment and avoids paying taxes while it grows. Taxes on the growth may be long-term capital gains taxes. For most of us today, that is 15% per year. Taxes on the growth could be paid at much higher marginal income tax rates if the investment generates short-term capital gains. Short-term capital gains occur when the investment is held less than one year or if it pays dividends.

Marge, Lorna and Dempsey

Let's look at three folks: Marge, Lorna, and Dempsey. All of them have $2,000 of income that they would like to invest. We will assume the investment is going to earn 10% per year consistently. Everyone's income is taxed at a marginal tax rate of 35%.

Marge will invest and not worry about taxes, instead paying taxes at marginal income tax rates every year. Lorna will pay income tax the first year, and then her investment is taxed at the long-term capital gains rate of 15%. Dempsey defers taxes.

Marge, Lorna and Dempsey

Marge	Pays Marginal Taxes
Lorna Pays	Long-term Capital Gains Taxes
Dempsey	Goes Tax Deferred

Marge and Lorna pay taxes on the $2,000 of income at their marginal tax rate of 35% and invest the difference. Here is what their initial investments look like:

Beginning Investment After Taxes

	Income to Invest	Less Taxes	Beginning Investment
Marge	$2,000	- $700	$1,300
Lorna	$2,000	- $700	$1,300
Dempsey	$2,000	$0	$2,000

Dempsey, with $2,000 compared to Marge and Lorna's $1,300, has a bigger initial investment. Unfortunately, this is about as far as most people and some tax accountants take the analysis. They simply ask: "Would you rather pay taxes or defer taxes?" For many folks, the answer is a resounding "defer!"

The disadvantages of tax deferral are often underestimated and the available tax free options are misunderstood. The chart below summarizes how our friends' investment account statements read over the next 30 years. Why is this chart not a fair comparison?

Time Compounds Tax Differences

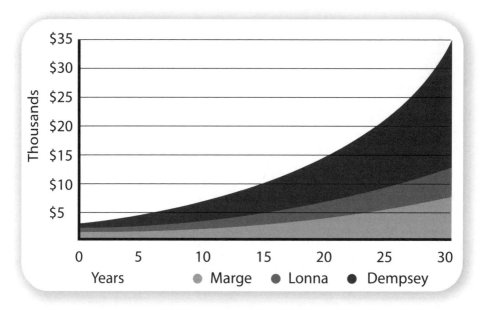

Here are some key years pulled out from the chart. Over a 30-year time horizon, Dempsey has a much larger amount of money than either of his two friends.

Key Years for Marge, Lorna & Dempsey

Year	Marge	Lorna	Dempsey
0	$1,300	$1,300	$2,000
5	$1,781	$1,955	$3,221
10	$2,440	$2,939	$5,187
15	$3,343	$4,420	$8,354
20	$4,581	$6,646	$13,455
25	$6,276	$9,993	$21,669
30	$8,599	$15,026	$34,899

Later, when the three friends use the money in their accounts, Dempsey has a fat tax burden, but Marge and Lorna have already paid their taxes. In other words, our comparison is unfair until we account for Dempsey's tax burden. Unfortunately, most of us look at our tax-deferred accounts without considering Uncle Sam's share. We forget that the initial $2,000 investment Dempsey makes from his income is actually funded by $700 of Uncle Sam's money. By deferring the taxes due today, Dempsey compounds his tax burden.

Let's assume that Dempsey pays taxes in any of the following years. The tax-deferred investment makes the most sense the longer Dempsey defers the burden. The following table illustrates Dempsey's after-tax advantage over Marge and Lorna.

After-Tax Advantage for Dempsey

Year	Marge	Lorna	Dempsey After-Tax
0	$1,300	$1,300	$1,300
5	$1,781	$1,955	$2,094
10	$2,440	$2,939	$3,372
15	$3,343	$4,420	$5,430
20	$4,581	$6,646	$8,746
25	$6,276	$9,993	$14,085
30	$8,599	$15,026	$22,684

Stretch the Deferral to Your Kids and Grandkids

One of the most exciting (and sometimes exaggerated) areas of financial planning is the "stretch" feature of qualified tax-deferred vehicles. A "stretch" is the ability for the living beneficiary of a qualified tax-deferred account to withdraw only the minimum amount of money over his or her life expectancy. Most IRAs and commercially sold annuities enable the stretch for two generations. This prolonged tax deferral adds up to a lot of money.

Which would you prefer: a tax-deferred account or taxable account? If you could stretch a tax-free account, wouldn't you be better off? Yes, in fact you would, and so will generations of your family.

You can see why the vast majority of tax accountants, financial professionals, and annuity companies promote tax-deferred investments. This level of analysis is where the fundamental launch point of this book begins because well-intentioned Dempsey will encounter a number of unintended consequences down the road.

SEP IRA

The SEP IRA is a special IRA for self-employed people and small business owners. The contribution limits are much higher than traditional IRAs and the benefits can be substantially greater. All money that goes into a SEP is an employer contribution. The owner must include employees who have worked three of the last five years, at least 500 hours per year. The owner must make the same percentage contributions for the employees as he does for himself.

The maximum annual contribution, in 2013, is $51,000 and/or 25% of compensation.

Simple IRA

A Simple IRA is different from other IRAs. It is also a plan for self-employed and small business owners with fewer than 100 employees. Unlike the SEP, the employee decides how much money goes into a Simple IRA. The employer is required to either put in a 2% non-elective contribution or match the employee's contribution up to 3% of his salary every year. All employees who received at least $5,000 of compensation in the past two years must be included in the Simple IRA. Finally, it is a "calendar year plan" that requires 60-day notice to employees before the employer can close the Simple Plan.

The maximum contribution in 2013 is $12,000 plus $2,500 catch-up for employees age 50 or older. A participant is required to hold the plan for two years before it can be rolled over.

And Why Not?

Choosing a tax-deferred IRA saves money over paying taxes as you go. Several reasons this may not work for you include:

You Have Other Deferred Assets

Instead of starting another tax-deferred investment, you would rather diversify your tax risk. In this case, you should look at the tax-free investment ideas.

Your Income or Age is Too High

If your income passes the thresholds for contributions, or you are over the age of 70 ½, then adding money to an IRA is not feasible except through a rollover. If you have not already consolidated your IRAs into a single account, you may consider that instead.

SEP IRA and Simple IRA Shortcomings

The SEP IRA for a small business owner requires owners to make the same percentage contribution into her employee's accounts as she gives herself. This gets expensive quickly. The Simple IRA is an oxymoron—difficult in comparison to the other IRAs, Simple IRAs operate under a completely different set of rules. Neither of them offers a tax-free option.

You Want to Go Tax Free

If you are sure that tax rates will be higher in the future, if you plan on compounding your investments, if you are fairly certain that your deductions will decline, then you are likely better suited for a Roth IRA, discussed in the next chapter.

Go Tax Free in a Roth IRA

CHAPTER 2

Absolute: Tax-deferred is tax-compounded, or you haven't grown your money.

Absolute: As we age, we frequently lose tax deductions.

Absolute: Future tax rates are likely to be higher, not lower.

How This Benefits Me

Know the rules, benefits and reasons for using Roth IRAs. Make an investment now that saves taxes later. Transfer tax-free wealth over three generations of your family.

Example

John and Angela are 63. John is a computer science engineer and, like many of his colleagues, he has worked at several companies. Angela, on the other hand, has been in management for the same company for the past 20 years. John accumulated most of his investments in tax-deferred IRA accounts. Angela, retiring this year, plans to roll her company 401k into her IRA. They plan to pull income from their IRA accounts every year for the rest of their lives. They are thankful that, over the years, they also accumulated a sizable amount of money in Roth IRAs because they can spend the Roth money with no future tax burden. John calls it "factoring in a zero" when he does his income tax return. The Roth IRAs are his favorite accounts.

What is a Roth IRA?

In many ways, a Roth IRA is easier to understand than the traditional IRA. Unlike a traditional IRA, a Roth doesn't offer a tax deduction on contributions. Instead, you pay taxes now and enjoy a tax-free income in retirement as long as you:

- Hold the Roth for at least five years and
- Take distributions no sooner than reaching age 59½.

Let's look at a few unique features of the Roth IRA.

The Five Year Clock

Roth IRAs (not Roth contributions) must be held for at least five years before the first withdrawal can be made, or the IRS will assess a 10% penalty. The first dollar into the Roth IRA starts the clock for all the money in the Roth IRA. Later contributions are subject to the same five-year clock as the first contribution. This is an important and often misunderstood distinction. You could put $1,000 in a Roth IRA and five years later make a $1 million Roth conversion (see chapter three), and all the money would be penalty and income-tax free.

Early Withdrawal Rules

An early withdrawal causes income tax on earnings. If this withdrawal is made prior to age 59½, it is also subject to a 10% federal tax penalty. Similar to the traditional IRA, a Roth allows penalty-free early withdrawals made for qualifying medical expenses, health insurance premiums, higher education expenses, a first-time home purchase, death, or disability.

Three Generation Stretch

Up to three generations of your family can avoid income tax in your Roth IRA. Your child or grandchild inherits your Roth IRA and, instead of spending it immediately, creates an "inherited IRA." They, too, enjoy tax-free growth (and access to) their money over their lifetimes!

Your generation, the first generation, avoids required minimum distributions (RMDs) entirely in a Roth IRA. The second and third generations of inherited Roth IRAs do have RMDs according to the inheritor's age. The inherited Roth IRA RMD comes out income-tax free.

Roth Contribution Limits

You may contribute to a Roth IRA as long as you report adjusted gross income below the required thresholds. The following table summarizes the adjusted gross income limits for 2013.[xi]

IRA Contribution Income Limits

2013	Single	Married Filing Jointly
Eligible	Less than $112,000	Less than $178,000
Contribution Gradually Phased Out	$112,000 to $127,000	$178,000 to $188,000
Not Eligible to Contribute	$127,000 or more	$188,000 or more

The annual contribution limits for a Roth are the same as a traditional IRA: the lesser of your taxable compensation for the year and $5,500 per person with an additional $1,000 available for people over 50. The per-person annual contribution limit applies no matter how you split it up, whether it is in one account, among many Roth IRAs, or traditional tax-deferred IRAs. The contribution limit applies to the total contribution into all IRAs.

What happens if you are married and your spouse is also employed? Each member of a working couple may make his or her own contribution.

Unlike a traditional IRA, the Roth does not require minimum distributions at any age, and contributions may be made after the age of 70½ as long as the account holder or spouse reports sufficient earned income.

Tax-free vs. Tax-deferred Math

Let's start with the numbers. Let's look at an investment. Let's say that this investment doubles in value every X number of years. Over six time periods, $1 grows to $64. Holding taxes constant, the tax burden also compounds at the same rate.

Had you paid taxes on this money the first year and then invested in a Roth IRA, never taxed again, you would have the exact same amount of money.

Tax-Free vs. Tax-Deferred Over Time

Period	Deferred	Tax	After Tax		Roth
0	$1.00	($0.30)	$0.70	=	$0.70
1	$2.00	($0.60)	$1.40	=	$1.40
2	$4.00	($1.20)	$2.80	=	$2.80
3	$8.00	($2.40)	$5.60	=	$5.60
4	$16.00	($4.80)	$11.20	=	$11.20
5	$32.00	($9.60)	$22.40	=	$22.40
6	$64.00	($19.20)	$44.80	=	$44.80

The key differences between tax-deferred and tax-free are the critical assumptions that we make. The assumptions we make often begin and end with indifference. As the next chapter shows, that's an expensive mistake.

Why Roth?

Many of us save for retirement in tax-deferred investment vehicles like 401ks, IRAs, SEP IRAs, Simple plans and others. Our retirement accounts are a well-deserved reward after a lifetime of hard work.

We feel stress over paying taxes, but we are thankful that we have deferred taxes until now, and that is at least a little comforting. But I'm going to make you uncomfortable. The truth is you have much more choice and control over how and when you are taxed than you thought. And, if you are deferring taxes, you are likely making a choice to pay more than you could be.

We are going to look at three absolute threats to choosing only tax-deferred investing. To the best of my knowledge, these cannot be disputed. Take these to heart and dwell upon them. You may already know these facts but you may not have thought about them in this way. You likely have not paid attention to them. Remember, tax is the single largest cost retired Americans pay.

Tax Compounded

Tax deferral is not enough. We love tax deferral because it looks like we have accumulated more money to spend. But the fundamental truth is that we have not accounted for taxes.

The first absolute threat to choosing only tax-deferred investing is that tax deferred is tax compounded. It has to be that way or you have not grown your money. Think about it. Holding taxes constant, this must be the case or you have not grown your money.

Let's look at an example. I pay you $50,000 for your hard work and we assume you will be taxed at the income tax rate of 35%. You are about to take $17,500 out of your pocket and give it to Uncle Sam. Now, I give you a choice. You can defer all $50,000, and defer the tax burden, or you can pay the taxes now and invest the remaining $32,500 in a never-again-taxed investment. Which would you prefer? Many of us would defer the taxes and compound the entire $50,000.

Remember, holding taxes constant, tax deferred is tax compounded. Over your 30-year retirement journey, using a long-term average stock market rate of return, you have taken the smaller initial tax amount and turned it into ten times more owed. Now which would you rather pay, $17,500 or $176,906? Which would Uncle Sam rather have you pay?[xii]

How is Uncle Sam going to pay for underfunded Social Security?

The answer (partially) lies in our retirement accounts. Uncle Sam knows how old we are, knows how much money we have, and really wants that money to grow. So, go stock market go, if nothing else than to pay for our own Social Security checks!

Now look at the next question: Why does this example hold taxes constant? Won't I go into a lower tax bracket in retirement years than I was while I was working?

Lost Tax Deductions

The second big threat to only choosing tax-deferred investments is that, as we age, we often lose tax deductions. As it has been, so it will be. Popular since the 1950s, a 30-year mortgage was designed to end when we reach retirement age so we could enter retirement with fewer financial burdens. Today, many folks carry a mortgage through their retirement years if, for no other reason, than to get a tax deduction. The mortgage interest deduction is one of the largest deductions enjoyed by average Americans today and, by design, it disappears for many of us as soon as we enter retirement.

So do other broad categories of tax deductions. As we raise our kids, we enjoy tax deductions, dependencies, tax exemptions, and tax credits. But if we send them to college, and if they return home like so many of them are now doing, we no longer get to count them on our tax returns.

A third category of tax deductions disappears by definition when we enter retirement: business-related expenses. By definition, when we enter retirement we have left the business. Many folks keep some sort of self-employed income in retirement years because they want more choice and control over their taxes.

Finally, while we are working, we are keeping ourselves in artificially low tax brackets with IRA, 401k, and other qualified retirement plan deductions. By definition, when we enter retirement, we lose these deductions. Our spending levels may stay the same, but our deductions decrease.

Many folks planning to enter a lower tax bracket in retirement may be planning to fail. Tax deferred is tax compounded. Holding taxes constant, it has to be that way or we haven't grown our money. Secondly, we often lose tax deductions as we age. The third threat to choosing only tax-deferred investing you already know. Let's look at the threat of future tax rates next.

Future Tax Rates

Do you think future tax rates are going to be lower, about the same, or higher?

When I ask this question in front of a crowd, I inevitably get a large number of head nods and occasionally strong opinions about the likelihood of higher tax rates in the future. This is the key question to ask:

Are you choosing to pay more in taxes than you have to?

If you choose to defer your taxes, grow the investment, then pull out the taxes on a larger amount of money, later in life, with fewer tax deductions and at higher tax rates, are you not choosing to pay more in taxes than you have to? Tax deferral is not enough. We must diversify our tax risks.

Have you looked at it in this way before? Do you feel uncomfortable? Do you really need a calculator, computer, or any math at all? These are the fundamental challenges American retirees face.

Safety, Control and Generosity

Where is your money safer: in the account that depends upon a future tax rate decrease, or in the account that has no future tax burden?

The account with no future tax burden has no obligation to the government. A tax-free account grows in value as tax rates rise, particularly compared to tax-deferred accounts.

Would you rather be in control or have the government in control?

The tax-free account puts you in the driver's seat. You may use any of the money at any time, regardless of what income tax bracket you may be in, regardless of the economy, and regardless of national and global politics and demographics. In the tax-deferred account, however, you worry about all of these things because they all threaten to increase your future and present tax rates and decrease your spendable money.

Would you rather transfer money to your children with or without taxes?

A tax-free account enables your children to inherit the money income tax free. Compared to a tax-deferred account, this can be a huge windfall for the folks you love. Compound the tax burden over the life expectancies of your children and grandchildren and you will see why we would all rather transfer (and inherit) tax-free money than tax-deferred money.

The Elusive Lower Tax Brackets

Let's look at the math for two families at different income levels. The numbers are not onerous, I promise!

The Centuries

Let's look at a family, the Centuries. The statisticians call the Centuries' $100,000 income "above average" but they and their neighbors call themselves middle class.

Looking back at the 2013 marginal tax rules, the Centuries are in the 25% tax bracket. If that is the case, the Centuries can earn another $46,400 in taxable income before they jump into the next tax bracket, where they will owe an additional 3% on every dollar they earn.

However, once they enter retirement, the Centuries, who diligently invested in tax-deferred investments, must cut their taxable income by nearly 28% in order to qualify for that lower tax bracket, 15%. This is either unrealistic, or it is a real failure.

Centuries Family's Income Brackets

High Point	$146,400
Today's Income	$100,000
Low Point	$72,500
Diff. High	$46,400
Diff. Low	$27,500

To minimize their taxes in retirement, the Centuries have two choices: A) plan on a frugal retirement, put as much money as they can in tax-deferred plans and perhaps spend all their money now, or B) plan on moving more money into tax-free retirement vehicles that enable them to have tax-free income.

The first choice is planning to fail, isn't it? Planning on a lower retirement tax bracket and continuing to sock money away in tax-deferred plans is counterintuitive. One defeats the other. You can see how tax-deferred plans increase taxes in retirement; they do not reduce them.

The second choice, moving more money into tax-free investment vehicles, is potentially a better choice for Americans who are serious about retirement.

The Centuries have a big set of challenges ahead of them as they try to move into a lower tax bracket in retirement. They cannot drop into the next lower tax bracket because it is (purposefully) too far away.

The Borderlines

Let's look at a family who is right on the cusp of two tax brackets and see how much they might actually save. Let's call them the Borderlines. They have a $150,000 taxable income and are currently just barely in that 28% tax bracket. In retirement, they hope to drop a tax bracket, and guess what? Their dreams come true. They fall into a lower tax bracket. Did it work?

During the Borderlines' 30 years of employment, they accumulate $100,000 of retirement savings. Add as many zeros as you like to make yourself feel comfortable. During those 30 years, they deferred taxes and saved $28,000 of taxes otherwise spent. Now they are in retirement. They go to withdraw that money and they are taxed at the next lower tax rate. They only have to pay 25% on each of their investments so they save 3% in taxes.

The Borderlines have made at least three critical bets that they have not fully explored.

Bet #1: Taxes Will Not Rise

First, the Borderlines are betting 3% of their retirement that the government will not raise taxes by 3% by the time they make those withdrawals. Unfortunately, history is against them. The federal government could quickly raise taxes again, just like they did in January 2013, with the passage of the American Taxpayer Relief Act.

Bet #2: Inflation Will Not Rise

Second, the Borderlines are betting against inflation. If tax brackets stay the same, if nothing else changes, or even if taxes go down, inflation marches along. In fact, inflation averages above 3% per year over long periods of time.[xiii] This means that approximately every 24 years, costs double. If the Borderlines want to preserve hope that their retirement tax savings are going to be taxed at a lower rate than before, they better hope that the federal government indexes the marginal tax rates for inflation.

Unfortunately, history once again sides against our family. Not only do they face paying the marginal tax, a second tax system called the alternative minimum tax (AMT) may eliminate their deductions. The Borderlines and many other

Americans face a two-headed hydra: if tax does not get them, inflation will.

Bet #3: I Won't Feel Bad

Third, the Borderlines are not accounting for the emotional cost of paying taxes when they are living off a fixed income. The Borderlines worry about the increased costs of medicine, of healthcare, of long-term care. But they have not considered the emotional cost of an increased tax burden as well.

The number one cost for the Borderlines—who successfully drop into a lower tax bracket, and who are doing about as well as the qualified plan can do for anyone—is the federal income tax they have diligently, assiduously deferred. Perhaps the second greatest cost is sales tax, and then perhaps a state income tax, and then it may become long-term gains as they sell assets to provide for emergencies.

At least three historical forces conspire against the tax-deferred investor. Many people believe the federal government is likely to raise tax rates, inflation marches on, and, as we age, the more likely we are to feel more financial stress. Families who defer their tax burdens until their retirement years defer their stress until later years. Unless, of course, they can earn tax-free income like in a Roth IRA.

A Nice Old Guy I Know

Sometimes an allegory says it best. So turn on your imagination.

Think of an elderly person who you either take care of now or you might have to care for someday. Imagine the moment when this person is completely dependent upon you for his or her care. This person is dependent upon you alone. No one else can help. You care for this person immensely.

Now you have two choices. Either you pay for this person's care or you do not. If you do not pay for this person's care, the care will not happen. Although it will cause you some discomfort, you can afford it.

Every decade, the cost to care for the nice old guy or gal doubles. A walker that costs $100 today reduces your account 20 years from now by $400.

Instead of a walker, imagine it is a tax bill. Would you prefer to have already paid $100? Or would you prefer to pay four times that much in the future, when you may be on a fixed income?

Phrased this way, it is an ethical imperative that you pay a little today instead of deferring your burden to the future. You will inflict much greater harm by deferring the problem than by swallowing today's tax pill.[xiv]

Remember this nice old guy. We return to him at the conclusion of this book.

And Why Not?

The Roth IRA is not for everyone. As tempting as it sounds, it is still one tool in a toolbox. Reasons not to fund Roth IRAs include:

Income

If your income is above the contribution limits, then you cannot make a Roth contribution. However, the Roth conversion, Roth 401k, and other options have no income limits and share the same tax-free benefits.

You Have a Short Time Horizon

If you will use the money in less than five years, then the benefits of the Roth IRA are null and void. Remember, however, that any small contribution into the Roth IRA starts the five-year clock. So, you could put in a small amount of money today and then, if you surpass your five-year window in spite of your plans, you can contribute a larger amount later. A longer time horizon gives you greater tax and investment advantages.

Your Beneficiary is a Charity

If your goal is to make a large gift to a favorite charity, then consider leaving the organization your traditional tax-deferred IRA and not a Roth IRA. A qualified charity can sell tax-deferred investments and spend the money with a zero income tax burden. A tax-deferred IRA is a bigger gift to a tax-exempt organization than it is to a child or grandchild.

You Are Already Retired

"I am already retired," is one reason. Here is another: "It's too late for me to make a Roth contribution." This may be true; if neither you nor your spouse have earned income from a job then you cannot contribute to a Roth IRA. However, you can still do a Roth conversion, discussed in the next chapter.

Go Tax Free in a Roth Conversion

Absolute: Long-term thinking costs money in the short-term and makes more money over the long-term.

Absolute: Short-term thinking makes money today and yields less over time.

How This Benefits Me

Learn the fundamentals of how and when to do a Roth conversion. See the $600,000 mistake made by many $100,000 investors. Decide whether you or your beneficiaries will benefit, how much you want the benefit to be, and how to undo a conversion.

Example

Bob and Sandy, in their 50s, may or may not ever receive an inheritance and they prefer to be financially independent. They have raised three children and are expecting their first grandchild. Now they want to leave their grandkids an inheritance, and they decide to perform a Roth conversion. Upon their passing, their grandchildren will each receive an income-tax free check from Bob's and Sandy's Roth IRA accounts every year, for the rest of their lives.

Roth Conversion

To convert to a Roth IRA, you will create a tax burden due at the end of the tax year. Each dollar of the conversion is added to your marginal tax bracket, paid at the same time as your regular income tax filing.

Working Your Bracket

You do not need to convert an entire IRA. Instead, you could convert only a portion. For example, a family could convert just enough to avoid moving into the next bracket.

Married Filing Joint	
Taxable Income	$100,000
IRA Amount	$500,000
Next Tax Bracket	$146,400
Conversion This Year (w/o hitting next bracket)	$46,400

It is typically a good idea for folks in the middle tax brackets to consider converting their IRAs slowly. This is a complicated choice. Folks in the highest marginal tax brackets might as well convert sooner rather than later if they fear tax rates will rise in the future, among the other reasons previously discussed.

Conversion to a Roth IRA provides several unique advantages, not the least of which is the peace of mind associated with a tax-free retirement income. We eliminate required minimum distributions. And, of course, the tax-free benefits stretch two more generations after us.

How Do I Convert?

Regardless of your age, there is no penalty when you convert your traditional IRA into a Roth IRA. While you will owe income tax on the amount converted, future earnings in the Roth IRA accumulate tax-free. You do not need to convert the entire traditional IRA amount into a Roth IRA, and you may perform separate conversions over different years to maximize your tax advantages.

Generally speaking, you will benefit from a Roth conversion if one of the two following statements is true:

• You have enough money outside of the IRA to pay taxes due upon conversion.
• You are over the age of 59½.

If you are under the age 59½, then you want to pay the taxes on the conversion with outside dollars.

Oops! Re-characterization!

If you change your mind shortly after you perform a Roth conversion, you can reconvert (in the same calendar year) and eradicate your tax burden. You can only reconvert once. Reasons to reconvert may include:

Investment losses: If you have a loser, you can reconvert and try again the next calendar year.

Tax bracket: You may have accidentally pushed yourself into a higher tax bracket. Business owners with good years, or saleswomen with great years or big bonuses, can find themselves in a position where they will be in a higher tax bracket than they expected.

Any reason at all: You can have a change of heart and re-characterize within the same calendar year for any reason at all.

Why Would I Convert?
A Simple Example

To calculate the advantages of a Roth conversion, we will perform three simple steps:

1. Estimate future traditional IRA values, tax obligations and RMDs.
2. Reinvest the RMDs.
3. Compare the sum of steps 1 and 2 with a Roth.

To keep things simple, we will make several assumptions:

- Marginal federal and state tax total is 30% in all years.
- Investments earn the same 10% rate of return.
- Taxable accounts are taxed as they grow at the marginal income tax rate.

Note that the underlying fundamental benefits could remain true even if the tax rate and rate of return are different than these assumptions. We do not consider loss years, a tax-loss carry forward, or other complex tax situations. For reasons discussed elsewhere, we do not assume a person will fall into a lower tax bracket, nor do we assume that the state or federal government will raise taxes.

Fred and Frieda, Sam and Samantha

Let's look at two couples at age 65. Fred and Frieda own a $100,000 traditional IRA and a $30,000 taxable account. Sam and Samantha own a $100,000 Roth IRA. Who has more money?

Who Has More Money?

	Fred and Frieda	Sam and Samantha
Traditional IRA	$100,000	$0
Taxable Account	$30,000	$0
Roth IRA	$0	$100,000

It appears Fred and Frieda have accumulated $30,000 more than Sam and Samantha. However, Fred and Frieda must pay taxes at his marginal income tax rate on any distributions made from his traditional IRA. At 30%, that's a $30,000 tax obligation. If Fred and Frieda were younger than 59½, he would actually have 10% less than that because of the early withdrawal penalty.

Surprisingly, when we consider taxes, the sum of their money is the same.

Sum is the Same At the Start

	Fred and Frieda	Sam and Samantha
Traditional IRA	$100,000 − $30,000 Taxes $70,000	$0
Taxable Account	$30,000	$0
Roth IRA	$0	$100,000
Total	$100,000	$100,000

Both couples have the same usable amount of money at the start of our hypothetical example. Fred and Frieda have $70,000 plus $30,000 in an outside taxable account, for a total of $100,000. Sam and Samantha have $100,000 in a Roth, where he has no tax obligation because he has already paid his taxes.

We must be careful to compare "apples and apples" when comparing a traditional IRA and a Roth. We may only count the after-tax spendable dollars; otherwise, we are not conducting a fair comparison. Fred and Frieda could set up a Roth just like Sam and Samantha at any time. But they do not appreciate the long-term costs of staying tax deferred or they are unable to get over the initial tax-cost hurdle.

At age 65, the two couples invest all of their money in accounts earning 10% per year. After one year, Fred and Frieda's traditional IRA grows to $110,000. He owes 30% in taxes so the after-tax value is $77,000. Fred and Frieda's taxable account grows 10% to $33,000 but that account is taxed as it grows (at their 30% marginal tax rate) so the net after-tax value is $32,100. The sum of their after-tax net spendable money is $109,100.

One Year Later

	Fred and Frieda	Sam and Samantha
Traditional IRA	$110,000	$0
	- $ 33,000 Taxes	
	$ 77,000	
Taxable Account	$33,000	$0
	- $ 900 Taxes	
	$32,100	
Roth IRA	$0	$110,000
Total	$109,100	$110,000

Sam and Samantha's Roth IRA grew 10% to $110,000. The Roth conversion earned Sam and Samantha an additional $900 in the first year. If Fred and Frieda understood this, they could convert his traditional IRA into a Roth IRA and use their taxable account to pay his tax obligation, and be on the same foot as Sam and Samantha. However, in our example, Fred and Frieda do not know this and the differences continue to compound.

The Next Three Years

	Fred and Frieda	Sam and Samantha	Roth Advantage
Age 67	$119,047	$121,000	+ $1,953
Age 68	$129,921	$133,100	+ $3,179
Age 69	$141,811	$146,410	+ $4,599

In a few short years, Sam and Samantha accumulate $4,599 more than Fred and Frieda by simply repositioning assets for a lesser tax burden. Now Fred and Frieda must make a required minimum distribution, and that increases the Roth advantage.

Fred and Frieda take out only the required minimum distribution amount using the RMD divisor found in IRS Uniform Lifetime Table 3, or 27.4. The value of the IRA prior to distribution is $161,051. The RMD is the IRA divided by the divisor, or $5,878. This leaves $155,173 in his traditional IRA after the distribution at the end of the year.

The $5,878 RMD is taxed at his income tax rate of 30%, or $1,763, which leaves $4,114. They invest this money in a taxable account.

Fred and Frieda also have a taxable account that started the year with a value of $39,324 and grows, net of taxes, to $42,076 by the end of the year. The following table summarizes the net values for both couple's accounts at the end of the fifth year.

Five Years Later

	Fred and Frieda	Sam and Samantha
Traditional IRA	$155,173 - $48,315 Taxes $108,621	$0
Taxable account	$43,256 - $1,180 Taxes $42,076	$0
RMD Taxable account	$5,878 - $1,763 Taxes $4,114	$0
Roth IRA	$0	$161,051
Total	$154,812	$161,051

The Roth advantage in the first year of required minimum distributions is $6,239. The advantage continues as the years go on because Sam and Samantha can earn the same rates of return as Fred and Frieda in a tax-advantaged arena, and they are not forced to pay taxes on the distributions. The chart shows that over 30 years, the Roth advantage adds up to $602,507.

A $600,000 Mistake

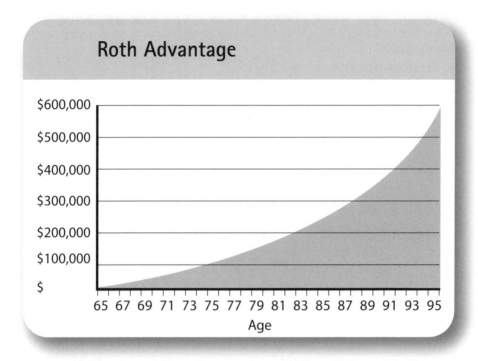

I call this the $600,000 mistake made by many $100,000 investors.

The couples were age 65 when they made the conversion. For younger couples, the differences are larger. For folks with larger amounts of money, the differences are larger. If you have children or grandchildren who will inherit these accounts, and stretch the tax-free benefits over their lifetimes, the differences are dramatically larger.

The assumptions are critical to understanding the right time to make a conversion.

The Roth Advantage

Many people make the mistake of treating all IRAs the same. However, as the hypothetical example shows, repositioning money into the proper vehicle yields a serious difference in investment amounts. Many people do not have enough information to make good decisions.

And Why Not?

Why not convert to a Roth IRA?

Ouch!

Paying taxes hurts. The psychological pain of giving away money immediately, even if over the long term it makes more money to do so, may be too much to bear. Money decisions are psychological as much as they are logical, and we must be honest about who we are and what we value.

Tomorrow's Losses

I may enter lower tax brackets in the future. I may have losses from a business or real estate or other financial anomaly that, if I combine them with my Roth Conversion, will mitigate my tax burden. In this case, it makes sense to defer until the same calendar year as the losses.

Complicated for Borderlines

Calculating the amount to convert depends upon your marginal income tax bracket for the year. Remember, you may not want to jump into a higher tax bracket unnecessarily. If your taxable income on any given year is near the threshold for the next higher bracket, then you may not want to do a conversion because it will bump you into that higher bracket.

I'm Too Old!

You may not want to do a Roth conversion late in life. You may not live to see the benefits. To do a Roth conversion at this stage of life would be an act of kindness for your beneficiaries.

None of us knows when it is our time. Your children will inherit your IRAs. They are likely in higher tax brackets than you are. You are fairly certain tax rates are going up in the future. Thus, your children will inherit IRAs with required minimum distributions payable at higher tax rates. If your investments grow, they will pay taxes on larger amounts of money. However, by choosing not to do a Roth conversion today, you have not had to pay the taxes today. Give this careful thought.

CHAPTER 4

Go Tax Free in a 401k with a Roth Option

Absolute: The best time to plant a tree is 50 years ago. The second best time is today.

How This Benefits Me

If you like the idea of a Roth IRA, then you may really like the idea of a Roth 401k. The annual contribution limits are significantly higher than a Roth IRA and, if you plan this correctly, you can convert even more money to tax-free Roth.

Example

Ken and Lisa own a small company that assembles and resells technology equipment. They have a small staff and a fairly large building. They would like to save money for themselves outside of the business which, on both an assets and income basis, puts them in a higher tax bracket. Ken and Lisa start a 401k plan with the Roth provision. Each of them max out their Roth contributions. They plan on future Roth conversions for the rest of their 401k accounts. They invest in conservative assets because, as Ken says, their company is their "risky equity investment."

Not Just for Big Companies

401k plans are not just for big companies! Solo 401k plans follow templates that allow sole proprietors and spouses to set up low-cost, easy-to-manage retirement plans. The big advantages of 401k plans for small companies include:

- Higher contribution limits than IRAs.
- More choice and control over when and how you are taxed.

A common mistake small business owners make is to assume that setting up a 401k plan is too expensive for them. The truth is that setting up a 401k plan has never been easier. Ongoing administration costs for IRS compliance can be nearly eliminated with the solo 401k option.

5500 Form and the IRS

If the company does not qualify for a solo 401k plan, then the company is forced to file another tax form. The 5500 form is a matter of public record and shows how much was contributed, number of participants, and other information. The administrator of the 401k plan, usually called a third party administrator (TPA) prepares the 5500 form and submits it to the IRS.

Non-discrimination Rules

401k plans are non-discriminatory, which means a business owner must make it available to everyone in the company. If the employer contributes money to his own account, then the employer needs to contribute a little money for everyone in the company, based on similar rules for all of them.

Vesting Schedule

The money that the employer contributes can be subject to a vesting schedule, rewarding loyal employees. Any money the employee elects to defer is not subject to the vesting schedule. Typical vesting schedules are 20% per year for five years; or after two years, 20% per year until the sixth year when employees are 100% vested.

401k Contribution Limits

The amount of money that an owner may contribute to a 401k plan is limited by the plan rules, and is divided into two categories, elective deferrals and employer contributions. The employee-contributed money is called an "elective deferral." In 2013, these dollars cannot exceed the following amounts:

• $17,500 or $23,000 if age 50 or older.
• The total contribution, including the company's contribution, cannot exceed $51,000 in 2013.

As you can see, you can contribute much more to a 401k plan than you can contribute to a stand-alone IRA, and this makes it especially appealing as a retirement savings vehicle.

Roth 401k

Employees can elect to contribute all of their contributions to a Roth 401k. Thus, Roth 401k contributions are limited to $17,500 per year.

Money that the company puts into the account on behalf of an employee must go into the tax-deductible, tax-deferred portion of the 401k. In other words, employer contributions cannot be put into the Roth portion of the 401k.

Roth 401k Conversion

A business owner who wants to move more money into the tax-free category could structure the 401k plan so that it allows in-force distributions or a Roth conversion. Any money converted to a Roth causes a tax burden for that calendar year. Roth gives you the advantages of tax-free growth of the money and no RMDs for non-owner employees.[xv]

Business owners should note this big difference between the Roth 401k and Roth IRA: The Roth IRA has no required distributions after age 70½. The Roth 401k does require distributions after age 70½ for owners of more than 5% of the company.

New in 2013

Now in 2013, a 401k participant can do a complete Roth conversion every year. This may invite an IRS audit because it has yet to be tested. Think about leaving money in the 401k for years and performing a Roth conversion when you can.

Safe Harbor 401k

A Safe Harbor 401k plan follows certain contribution rules for the employer that enable the highly compensated, and the owners, to maximize their 401k contributions. The Safe Harbor rules vary. One of the most common rules is that the employer provides the employee a 100% match on the first 3% of the employee's salary she contributes, and 50% on the next 2% of her contribution. This totals 4% of payroll.

From a business-owner standpoint, this sometimes seems expensive. Granted, employee benefits are a huge attraction for qualified talent in today's workforce, thus many employers feel compelled to create a 401k plan regardless of the costs. The question is: how can the employer owner get the biggest bang for his or her buck from the contribution?

All 401k plans require a financial professional. Many companies have off-the-shelf solutions for small business owners and start-up companies. The best advice comes from planners who specialize in the 401k marketplace.

Own Company Stock in a 401k

Many small business owners know their own business is their best investment. They look at a 401k and ask, "Why would I purchase anything else?"

Why not purchase your own business in your tax-deferred or tax-free Roth 401k?

For owners who are less than a 50% owner of a business, this might be a viable solution.

Many large corporations allow, and even encourage, their employees to purchase company stock inside their 401k retirement plans. Sometimes, employers provide a discount, usually around 15%, on the share price of the stock as an added bonus for employees. For everyone but the highly compensated and the business owner, a 401k does not require minimum distributions after age 70½ —a nice bonus for the rank-and-file!

The problem is that small business owners are excluded from these benefits. A greater than 50% owner cannot use his 401k or IRA to purchase shares in a business in which he, or any disqualified person, owns a 50% or greater share.

ESOP: Employee Stock Ownership Plan

The employee stock ownership plan (ESOP) is both complicated and beneficial for business owners. First, owners can sell their own shares to the people who have the most at stake in the business—employees. This can increase loyalty, motivate them to stay later and work harder, among other benefits. They provide significant tax benefits for today's owner, including a possible exit plan. An ESOP requires outside audits and an expert team to set up and maintain. To understand all of the rules is outside of our scope here. Suffice it to say, for owners not afraid of complications, ESOPs can be a great tool.

Net Unrealized Appreciation

Net unrealized appreciation (NUA) is a tax benefit of owning your own company stock in a 401k. When an employee leaves, she rolls the company stock into a taxable account. The NUA rule assures that she will only pay income tax on the original value of the stock. The rest of the gains since purchase price are taxed at the long-term capital gains rate. That's a unique bonus.

This works best for appreciated stocks. If the value of the stock is approximately the same as the purchase price, the former employee is better off rolling the entire amount into an IRA and avoiding the immediate tax hit.

Unrelated Business Income Tax

When an IRA owns an indebted business (like a real estate property), the IRS levies unrelated business income tax (UBIT). Owning that same property in a solo 401k can be one way to avoid this problem, which presents a whole list of other considerations. UBIT creeps outside the scope of this book, but it is important to understand the term. To structure a plan where a business is held inside a retirement plan requires an expert who can help you carefully consider the pros and cons, incentives, and ramifications.

Conclusion

Remember these fundamental rules about 401k retirement plans:

- Forced savings are good for employers and employees.
- The longer we live, the bigger the advantages are for tax-free investment choices.
- The Roth 401k allows larger contributions to the Roth vehicle than we can get anywhere else.
- The 401k plan allows larger contributions to tax-deferred investment vehicles than IRAs.
- Roth 401k conversions can be a way to move large amounts of deferred money into tax-free money.

And Why Not?

If you're considering setting up a 401k, remember:

Qualified Plans Are Complicated

Any plan qualified with the IRS is a complicated plan. The rules are subject to change and the business owner will want to spend time becoming comfortable with the language, rules, and professionals.

Non-Discrimination

Employers looking to maximize their own benefits may not be happy with giving more money away to their employees. The good news on this front is that your employees are your best assets. They are keeping the money. It is not a required expense without a direct measurable return.

Go Tax Free with an OUR Plan

Absolute: Lack of life insurance accounts for most of the poverty among widows and widowers.[xvi]

Absolute: Most life insurance is owned by the wealthiest among us—the folks who (you might think) need it the least. What can we learn from them?

How This Benefits Me

Life insurance based planning is among the most flexible and powerful vehicles available and offers significant benefits. The cash value accumulates without a tax burden, an array of investment options is available, and it creates a death benefit for a legacy.

Example

Bill owns a successful small business and wants to transfer it to a child. He knows his son is capable of running the firm but is not able to afford it. Bill sets up a life insurance based plan and puts in the maximum funds allowed by law. When Bill passes away, the death benefits pay off the business. While alive, Bill has access to the cash values of the life insurance without a tax obligation.

What is an Our Plan?

My firm, A & I Financial Services, coined the term "OUR plan." It stands for "optimized universal life insurance supplemental retirement plan." Before we dive into the details, we need to look at life insurance fundamentals, learn the vocabulary, and assess the pros and cons. Finally, we will look at how to structure an OUR plan.

Introduction

Life insurance is one of the most difficult financial planning concepts to understand. This lack of understanding coupled with confusing industry dynamics make it difficult to purchase. It is beyond the scope to do a proper analysis here of all of the different forms of life insurance. Instead, my goal is to help you make an educated decision about how a properly funded life insurance policy may fit into your financial plans.

Why Life Insurance?

The need for life insurance arises out of a concern for the people we love. A good place to start is with lost income. First, ask yourself this question: "How much income would be lost if I were to die today?"

Additional considerations are given to immediate needs such as college funding, burial expenses, emergency reserves, and debt. A competent financial professional should perform a family needs analysis to determine how much life insurance you need.

For example, a person earning $50,000 per year might purchase a policy with a death benefit of $833,333. An expected long-term after-tax rate of return might be 6%.

$50,000 divided by 6% is $833,333.

If we put this money into an account that earns 10% per year, the beneficiary would be able to pull 6% out during the first year ($833,333 times 6% = $50,000) leaving the remaining 4% to earn interest.

Lack of life insurance accounts for most of the poverty among widows and widowers.

This key truth was uncovered by a variety of economists in a variety of research projects, but is perhaps most succinctly stated in Boston University Economics Professor Larry Kotlikoff's research.[xvii]

Without delving into unnecessary numbers, think about why a lack of life insurance causes most of the poverty among widows and widowers. Death causes an income stream to disappear, Social Security benefits disappear, and a spouse and/or children face financial hardships. Without life insurance, the risk of death is carried by the family, not the insurance company. Without life insurance, a family skates on thin ice, hoping for the best.

Through the law of large numbers, actuaries, and risk management, the insurance company bears the financial risk of death, making it easier for the survivors to cope. It provides relief from financial worries at a time when families need it most. The death benefit of most life insurance policies is paid within 60 days from the date of death and includes interest payable up to that point. Many insurance companies offer various modes of payment including an annuity stream or a lump sum. The recipient of the death benefit does not pay income tax on the amount received.

A Unilateral Contract

A life insurance contract is frequently referred to as a unilateral contract. This means that most of the promises and stipulations are made by the insurance company which underwrites the contract. The consumer simply applies to the insurance company stating his or her health, age, and need for life insurance coverage. Once the life insurance company determines health and need status, the insurance company may make an offer to insure. The acceptance of this offer, along with payment, places the policy in force.

The only promises the consumer must abide by are to be honest on the application and to pay the premiums due. For two years after the date of acceptance there is a period of time during which the insurance companies can, at their discretion, challenge or contest a death benefit. For example, an insurance company could challenge a fraudulently induced contract in which the applicant misrepresented the facts on the original application. In some states, there is also a one or two-year window during which a death by suicide would forfeit the death benefit.

On the other hand, the insurance company has a very complex set of obligations. They must pool all the potential mortality obligations and carry enough reserves to meet those obligations. They must account for the contract. They need to report to the policy owner on a regular basis. They need to conduct their administrative operations. They need to invest wisely and maintain the minimum reserves required to meet death payment obligations. They need to maintain their reserves and operate with profitability at a level that will attract and retain clients.

Obligations

Unilateral Obligations	
Policy Owner	**Insurance Company**
Be honest on the application	Meet reserve requirements
Pay insurance premiums	Account for contracts
	Report to clients
	Pool and minimize risks
	Invest wisely
	Pay death benefits
	Maintain fair business operations
	Earn competitive rates of return
	Keep insurance costs competitive
	Fulfill regulatory requirements

After an insurance policy is issued, the insurance company will ask the agent to deliver the policy to the policyholder. Keep the physical insurance policy in a secure location and make sure that your estate executor knows where to find it.

Types of Life Insurance

Life insurance comes in two main forms:

1. Term insurance, lasting for a specific term.
2. Permanent insurance, lasting until death.

Permanent life insurance comes in two general types: whole and universal life.

Term Life Insurance

Term life insurance provides the applicant life insurance for the covered period of time with a guaranteed low premium payment for a certain number of years, usually 10, 15 or 20 years. Term life insurance disappears if the premium is not made. Upon completion of the guarantee period, the applicant usually has a renewable right, or the right to renew the policy at the adjusted (higher) premium payments. Most term life policies are also convertible to universal or whole life policies.

The benefits of term life insurance include low apparent out-of-pocket costs and high death benefits for the amount of premium. The downsides of term insurance are less apparent but, once understood, may outweigh the benefits. As an applicant ages, term insurance grows more costly. Typically, it is a dramatically large cost increase. This cost increase can cause financial hardships for the applicant.

Either one of two things happens to a term policy-owner as they age. Either A) the owner converts the term policy to a universal or whole life insurance policy, or B) the owner stops paying for life insurance and loses this protection. Unfortunately, the most common situation we see in our firm is that people drop the life insurance protection. As we get older, our need for life insurance may not decrease but the cost of term life insurance will likely increase a lot.

How does an insurance company make profits? One way is to eliminate its debt payments. When the insured drops a term life insurance policy, an obligation disappears from the insurance company's books, and the company has earned years of income without having to pay a death benefit. Term insurance makes insurance companies wealthy.

How can the insured earn great profits? We discuss one popular idea next: buy term and invest the difference. Let's look at this "common wisdom" approach.

Buy Term and Invest the Difference

If I can buy term insurance with a lower premium than a permanent life insurance policy, then I could invest the difference (in the stock market, corporate bonds—you name it) and potentially earn a better rate of return.

We can run a customized illustration for your situation, but we don't need to. The logic in the "buy term" argument depends upon a false assumption: excess premiums cannot be invested.[xviii]

We can invest the excess premiums inside the life insurance policy. The investments inside the policy are comparable to investments outside the policy.

We can earn comparable returns inside a permanent life insurance policy as we can earn in outside investments.

If we can earn the same return inside a policy that we can outside the policy (and we can), then the two investments are equal. If we have ample liquidity, there are significant benefits for investing within the policy rather than outside of it.

Inside a permanent life insurance policy, we have no future tax burden. Therefore, life insurance has a potentially larger after-tax value than the equivalent taxable investment. Plus, the policy pays a death benefit to our beneficiaries. Think this through completely and make sure you understand it whole-heartedly before you continue reading.

If two investments earn the same rate of return but one of them is taxed and one of them uses after-tax dollars and is not subject to income tax, the tax-smart investment has a substantially greater value. The return on a no-tax investment is always larger than the same return on a taxed investment. All things being equal, taxes reduce returns. If I do not have to pay taxes, I earn better returns.

Permanent life insurance grows tax-deferred, can be accessed tax-free, and upon death, transfers income-tax free. It is very difficult, if not impossible, to find another vehicle with the liquidity and income tax free benefits of life insurance.

Whole Life Insurance

Whole life insurance is a form of permanent life insurance. Some of the premium pays for mortality costs and the excess premium payments are invested income tax free. Whole life payments may be made over the entire life of the applicant, which (almost) guarantees the out-of-pocket costs to the applicant will not increase for life.[xix] Other policies can be paid over a certain number of years, usually twenty years, and are called paid up policies.

A few whole life products invest the cash value accumulations in variable accounts linked to stock market returns. Most whole life policies, however, invest this money in fixed, guaranteed-rate investments. Most policies provide the security that if a policy owner misses a payment, the payment is made from the cash value accumulation and the policy does not terminate.

If the policy owner wants to stop making payments to a whole life policy altogether, unlike the term life which completely disappears, a whole life policy offers the owners several options. One option is to convert to a reduced paid up policy, which offers a reduced death benefit guaranteed for life. The second option is to convert the policy into a paid-up term policy, which provides the same death benefit for a guaranteed length of time. The final option is to surrender the policy for the cash value less fees due.

Whole life provides certain benefits to the buyer, including a death benefit, some premium payment flexibility, and an accumulating cash value that can be accessed during a person's lifetime.

Universal Life

Universal life is the subject of the rest of this chapter. Universal life insurance provides permanent life insurance. Compared to whole life, universal life offers more investment options and more options for accessing the money in these accounts. Finally, universal life insurance enables the size of the death benefit to change.

A universal life insurance contract has two features that differentiate it from other types of life insurance:

- Flexible premium
- Adjustable life insurance benefit

Flexible premium means you may contribute more than required or less than required, depending upon your needs. In bad years, you may contribute the minimum or perhaps nothing at all: The insurance premium is paid for by the cash accumulation. In good years, you may contribute more than the maximum to take advantage of the policy's income tax-free accumulation.

The "adjustable life" portion of the definition of universal life insurance refers to the death benefit options. Just like the premiums can change, the death benefit can increase or decrease according to your needs. An increase in death benefits may require underwriting. Death benefit options account for a large amount of misconceptions, so I will discuss these in detail. First, we need to understand the three broad categories of investment options available in universal life insurance.

Three Types of Universal Life Insurance

Universal life insurance provides investment flexibility. Many of the same types of investments available outside universal life are available inside universal life, including fixed investments, variable investments linked to the stock market, or a hybrid, called equity-indexed investments.

Fixed Universal Life

Fixed universal life insurance credits a rate of return competitive with investment grade corporate bonds. Depending upon the insurance policy, these returns can be guaranteed for one year up to five or more years. Fixed insurance provides guaranteed growth of cash values free from fluctuations in the stock market. The money is kept in the company's general account and is guaranteed by the company's claims-paying ability.

Variable Universal Life

Variable universal life (VUL) insurance combines the features of variable and universal life insurance, giving you the control over investment options as well as the ability to adjust your premiums and death benefit. Variable universal life insurance is designed for individuals in need of permanent life insurance protection with an investment component. When you own a VUL policy, you can direct a portion of your net premium payments to any of the investment options available through the separate sub-accounts depending on the particular variable life product. Each investment option offers a different level of risk and growth potential.

Withdrawals may be subject to surrender charges and are taxable if you withdraw more than your basis in the policy. Policy loans or withdrawals will reduce the policy's cash value and death benefit, and they may require additional premium payments to keep the policy in force. There may also be additional fees and charges associated with a VUL policy.

Generally, policies have contract limitations, fees, and charges, which can include mortality and expense charges, account fees, underlying investment management fees, administrative fees, and charges for optional benefits. In addition, if a policy is surrendered prematurely, there may be surrender charges and income tax implications.

Variable universal life policies are not guaranteed by the FDIC or any other government agency; they are not deposits of, nor are they guaranteed or endorsed by, any bank or savings association. The investment return and principal value of an investment option are not guaranteed. Because variable universal life subaccounts fluctuate with changes in market conditions, the principal may be worth more or less than the original amount invested if it is surrendered.[xx]

Equity Indexed Universal Life

An increasingly popular form of insurance is a hybrid of the previous two types called equity-indexed universal life insurance (EIUL). The excess premium is kept in the general account of the insurance company and is guaranteed by the company's claims-paying ability. The insurance company then buys an investment vehicle called a call option. The option rises according to the value of a major stock market index, usually the S&P 500 Index. If the stock market gains in value, the EIUL account is credited the gain, the money is moved into the general account, and another option is purchased. If the stock market loses value, the option expires worthless and the insurance company purchases another call option.

Equity-indexed accounts earn a low fixed rate of return guaranteed by the insurance company (it might be 2%) regardless of how the stock market performs. Equity-indexed accounts participate in bull stock market rallies by earning up to a maximum rate of return, which might be 12%. A full discussion of equity indexed products is outside the scope of this book, but now you should have enough information to ask informed questions of your expert.

Investment flexibility is a key feature of universal life insurance. From fixed to variable, from very safe to rather aggressive, an insurance contract can be a powerful wealth generation and wealth preservation vehicle.

Living Benefits

To understand how universal life insurance works, consider the following diagram. It shows an investment that, over time, increases in value. An investment earns a rate of return, this money is reinvested, the earnings are compounded, and the money grows.

Cash Value of Any Investment

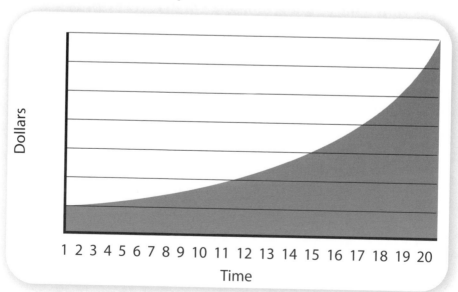

This diagram could show an investment in a mutual fund, real estate, an annuity, a certificate of deposit, or virtually any investment. Inside an insurance contract, this is called the cash value, and it provides living benefits. The cash value of an insurance policy is available to the owner while he or she is living. She can withdraw the money at any time, free from taxes, hence the phrase "living benefit." Living benefits form the first feature of universal life insurance. The second feature of universal life insurance is the death benefit.

Death Benefit Options

Most universal life insurance policies offer two death benefit choices. The choices are referred to either as Option A or Option B. Some companies will call them Option 1 and Option 2. Regardless of the nomenclature, the death benefits take either of two shapes, illustrated below. The solid gray area indicates the cash value accumulation over time. The striped area indicates the size of the insurance. The sum of these two areas is the benefit paid when the insured dies.

Cash Value: the amount of money in excess of cost of insurance that may be invested inside a permanent life insurance policy.

Universal Life Level Death Benefits

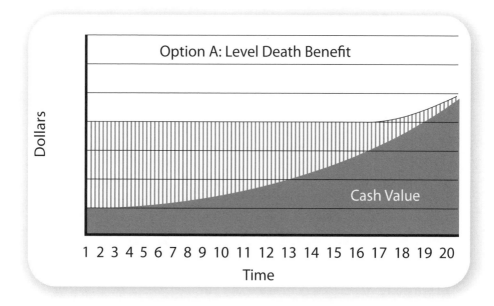

An Option A (Option 1) contract includes the cash value in the death benefit. Over time, the amount of pure insurance decreases as the amount of cash value increases. This insurance ramps up like a hockey stick in later years when the cash value grows very large. An insurance policy must keep a certain amount of "pure insurance" in order to maintain a tax-preferred status with the IRS. This amount is called the corridor. Thus, Option A is called a "level death benefit" policy, but the total death benefit may increase as the cash value approaches the amount of the death benefit.

The second option, shown next, provides for a rising insurance death benefit. Notice that the amount of pure insurance, in gray, remains constant over the years of the policy.

Universal Life Increasing Death Benefits

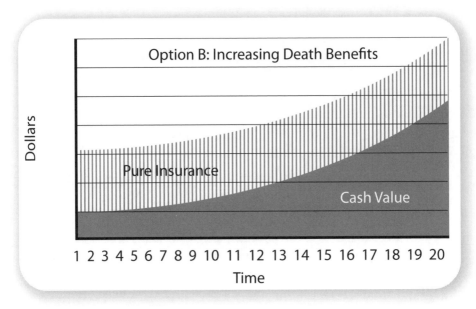

At first glance, it may seem like Option B is the best contract. Since the cash value is in addition to the pure insurance, the death benefit grows larger as the insured grows older. However, life insurance costs increase at older ages, slowing the growth rate of the cash value. Option A provides greater living benefits and Option B provides greater death benefits.

Note that the insurance company only charges a mortality cost (cost of insurance) for the exact amount of life insurance in the contract. The choice between insurance types is simply a matter of deciding whether living benefits outweigh the need for estate benefits. The ultimate use of the policy dictates the proper option for you (living benefits vs. estate benefits).

Funding

You can fund a universal life policy in various amounts according to your needs. Funding options are on a continuum, from minimum funded to maximum funded, as shown below.

Funding Options

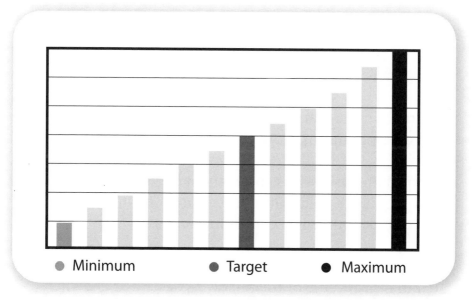

The insurance company creates a number, called the target premium, which is the company's best estimate at a safe funding level that will enable the policy to stay in force if you miss or need to delay a premium payment at some future date. How you choose to fund the policy determines the policy benefits.

A minimum-funded policy provides the highest death benefit per dollar. It has a higher chance of lapsing if you miss a premium payment. A minimum-funded policy provides the lowest cash value.

A maximum-funded policy provides the lowest death benefit per dollar of premium, and it provides the greatest protection if you miss a payment. A maximum-funded policy provides the highest cash value, or living benefit. A universal life insurance contract could be structured this way because of the tax benefits, described next.

Taxation

To understand the tax benefits of universal life insurance, it is important to understand these two features of universal life insurance:

- Premiums are larger than insurance cost.
- Excess premiums grow tax-free.

Universal life insurance is permanent life insurance, enabling you to put more dollars into the insurance contract than are needed to pay current life insurance costs.

The excess premium above the cost of the insurance becomes the initial cash value of the policy. As described elsewhere, cash value insurance takes one of three general types: fixed insurance, equity-indexed fixed insurance, or variable insurance. Depending upon the type of insurance, the cash value grows tax free, can be accessed tax free, and upon death, transfers to the policy beneficiaries income-tax free.

Insurance pays income-tax free benefits. Just like automotive insurance pays a tax-free benefit when the insured car is damaged, life insurance transfers an income-tax free death benefit to the beneficiary. You do not have to file an IRS income tax return every year your health insurance company pays for your medical care. Similarly, life insurance is income-tax free.

Because life insurance enables people to invest more money in the policy than is necessary to cover immediate insurance needs, the IRS imposes guidelines on the amount of money a person can put into a policy.

Why is this? If you have $1 million dollars and you could grow and use this money tax-free, why wouldn't you buy the smallest policy possible, as quickly as possible, and start to enjoy a tax-free retirement income?

That's exactly what many people want to do. To prevent abuse, the IRS requires at least these two features in a life insurance contract:

- Premium payments are made over a period of time.
- Some amount of risk must be transferred to the insurance company.

To understand why this is the case, let's look at an extreme example.

Let's say a person writes a check to an insurance company for $1,000,000 for a policy that pays a $1,000,001 death benefit. This is against the law because it breaks these two rules above.

The reason the IRS prohibits a person from buying a $1,000,001 policy with a $1 million dollar check is simple: the IRS is losing out on any future income taxation of that $1 million. The insurance company hasn't absorbed enough risk. The company has a $1 risk of the person dying. This is obviously an abusive tax shelter and not an insurance policy.

To avoid problems with the IRS, pay the right amount of taxes. To maximize your retirement, do not pay any more taxes than you are required.

Consult with an insurance and financial professional to look at funding options and timeframes. To maximize your retirement, work with a professional to structure your policy with the minimum death benefit. To maximize your estate, work with your insurance expert to fund your policy with a target premium or slightly less than target.

The OUR Plan

An optimized universal life insurance supplemental retirement plan, or OUR plan, is custom fit client by client.

To maximize your living benefits in retirement, consider structuring a universal life insurance policy with the minimum death benefit. No one objects to having life insurance, we only object to paying for it. To minimize the cost of life insurance, minimize the death benefit and maximum fund the policy in the shortest time allowed by the IRS. By structuring your insurance contract this way, you have created a vehicle with a large cash pool and no future tax burden.

To fund a retirement, or to pay for a grandchild's education, or to remove your money from the life insurance contract for any other reason, you may use either a withdrawal or a loan.

Withdrawals

Withdrawals from an insurance contract are made without tax burden up to the point of the original dollar investment. Accountants call this FIFO: First In First Out. This means that if you invest $100,000 in your insurance contract, and over time it's grown to $500,000, your first $100,000 can be withdrawn income tax free.[xxi]

The OUR plan is far more tax-efficient than qualified plans like IRAs, 401ks, and qualified or non-qualified annuities. These latter vehicles are taxed on a LIFO basis, or Last In First Out. This means that, in the same $500,000 example above, your first $400,000 of withdrawals would be taxed at your marginal income tax rate. Ouch!

Loans

The second way to withdraw money from an insurance contract is through a policy loan. When the money is withdrawn using a loan, the insurance company charges you an interest rate and then credits you the same or nearly the same interest rate. The result is a wash. Some insurance companies put this loan rate in writing. Others make a guarantee that the loan rate charged will never be more than ¼ of one percent above the interest rate credited to the account. Competitive forces in the industry keep companies' rates fairly comparable.

Do you pay income tax on a loan? No. Think about it. When you signed what is likely the largest loan your family has ever seen, your mortgage, did you have a huge income tax bill? Of course not. It is no different with a policy loan. You have no income tax burden. Plus, you have no obligation to pay off the loan while you are alive.

You do not have to pay off your insurance policy loan during your lifetime because the loan is paid off by the death benefit upon your death. Remember the two general ways to structure a life insurance contract discussed above, either Level A or Increasing B. In either event, you have loaned yourself your own money. The loan decreases the death benefit to your children or other beneficiaries; however, your beneficiaries will still receive the balance upon your death.

When you structure the plan for maximum living benefits, you may earn a tax-free income for life. Now what is wrong with that?

The Estate Plan

To maximize your estate, consider funding your policy with a target premium or slightly less than target. This type of plan benefits a person in either of the following two situations who:

- Wants to grow the amount of money left for the beneficiaries
- Wants to pay an estate tax burden

By far the most common way to structure policies is for a person to look at his or her beneficiaries and want to provide for them.

Life insurance gives a person the ability to say "I love you" from the grave. It provides for those who depend upon us even after our death. The level of life insurance a person carries can say a lot about the level of responsibility a person feels for his or her loved ones.

The second reason for a target or slightly-less than target plan is to minimize a person's out-of-pocket tax expense. The estate taxation system in the United States significantly impacts people who have accumulated wealth within their families. The least expensive way to provide a check for Uncle Sam is through life insurance. For pennies on the dollar of benefit, a person can provide his or her family a huge inheritance and provide Uncle Sam the legal estate taxes due.[xxii]

Choosing a Professional

Many consumers make the mistake of treating all insurance policies and insurance agents the same. However, as the hypothetical example shows, repositioning money properly for your unique situation yields significant benefits. These explanations are insufficient to inform you whether an OUR plan is the best choice for you.

As you look for a professional, one place to start is to find a member of the Million Dollar Round Table, or MDRT. This membership organization of life insurance professionals swears an oath to put their clients' interests ahead of their own and to act with the highest integrity. Learn more about them at www.mdrt.org. Another organization is the Financial Planning Association, www.fpanet.org. Although they are not exclusively life insurance producers, FPA members swear to uphold a strict code of ethics.

And Why Not?

Why not purchase life insurance?

Insurability

Someone needs to be insurable. Life insurance goes through an underwriting process. If the applicant does not meet the insurance company's health guidelines 1) the cost of insurance could be too high, or 2) the insurance company will deny life insurance. A denial will become part of the applicant's permanent health record.

Insurable interest

Someone needs to have an insurable interest on the insured person in order to own it. Without a true insurance purpose in addition to the tax-free cash value accumulation potential, this plan will not work.

Costs, Apparent and Hidden

Life insurance costs are different than many other investment vehicles. By working with life insurance professionals who pledge to adhere to a strict code of ethics, like the members of MDRT and FPA, you will be informed of the costs inside the policies you own and understand how life insurance supports your overall financial plan. Loans and partial withdrawals reduce the death benefit payable to your beneficiary. If your policy lapses with an outstanding loan, it will be treated as a distribution and some or all of the amount may be taxable.

Variable products are exposed to market risk, including the possible loss of principal. Variable products are sold by prospectus. Carefully consider the investment objectives, risks, charges, and expenses that may apply before investing. The prospectus contains this and other important information about the investment company. Read the product and underlying fund prospectuses carefully before investing. Ask many questions before you begin, and you will be best served and most satisfied.

Go Tax Deferred in an Annuity

"I'm more interested in the return OF my money than the return ON my money." Mark Twain

How This Benefits Me

Annuities provide a way to get tax-deferral on larger amounts of money outside of qualified plans like IRAs and 401ks. Annuities can also be owned inside IRAs and Roth IRAs. They provide unique guarantees, including (possibly) an income you cannot outlive, a guaranteed rate of return, and a death benefit (without underwriting), among others.

Example

Anne wants to stop worrying. She worries that she will outlive her money. She does not have a pension at work. She worries that her investments will lose money. She worries about inflation and taxes, too. Her mother lived to 102, and Anne is in far better shape than her mom was. Anne remembers her dad losing a lot of money once when she was younger. Anne is very good at many things, but she is sure that money is not one of them. She really doesn't even like it! Anne decides that an annuity from a large and respected insurance company is a perfect way for her to guarantee she will receive an income she will not outlive. With this peace of mind, she can rest easy about her other investments.

How an Annuity Works

Commercial annuities come in many different types and have many different features and benefits. Annuities can get complicated quickly, but, at its core, an annuity is easy to understand. Annuity means an annual payment.

Annuitant: The person on whose life the annuity is based.

Owner: The person who owns the annuity.

Note: The owner and annuitant can be different people.

Usually the owner is the annuitant. However, a person may want to have a separate annuitant as the owner. In Anne's case, she is both the owner and the annuitant.

Pretend Anne is married to Dick who cannot get life insurance. She owns the annuity and he is the annuitant. If Dick passes away, Anne gets a death benefit. These two words—annuitant and owner—are important.

Immediate Annuity

An immediate annuity starts an income stream immediately, guaranteed to last for life or for a certain period of time.

An immediate annuity is a good place to start to understand annuities. You write a check to an insurance company and the company promises to make payments to you. You can choose from many different periods:

• *Lifetime:* Regardless of how long you live, the annuity will make a fixed payment.

- **Period certain:** The annuity guarantees to make payments for a certain period of time whether you are alive or not. Typical periods include five, ten, and 20 years.

- **Lifetime or Period certain:** The annuity pays for the GREATER of a certain period of time or your lifetime. For example, you might choose lifetime or ten years, whichever is greater.

An immediate annuity pays larger payments on "lifetime only" annuities for older annuitants.

Deferred Annuity

Deferred annuity: A deferred annuity offers income guarantees that begin in the future, at a date that may or may not be determined by the annuitant at the start.

The deferred annuity has become more popular in recent years because the owner of the annuity can set aside money, tax-deferred, and invest the money in a variety of different vehicles. Later in life, the owner can choose the same income options as above, plus others described next. The deferred annuity offers an array of investment options, including:

- **Fixed annuity:** A fixed interest rate for the duration of the annuity. Sometimes these annuities offer a bonus (an additional percentage contribution to your account) in the first year or two.

- **Equity indexed annuity (EIA):** A crediting rate linked to a stock market (and sometimes bond or other market) index, and usually guaranteed not to lose money in a given year. Equity indexed annuities have many costs, features, and rules, and they get complicated quickly. Make sure you understand the various features of an EIA and how they work together. Ask your professional advisor questions about participation rates, spread, margin and asset fees, interest rate caps and all applicable fees, charges and expenses. Be sure to read the contract very carefully. You need to understand that an EIA is a long-term investment and it is possible to lose money in an EIA.

• *Variable annuity:* A crediting rate that could go up or down depending upon the performance of the underlying investments. The investments look and behave like mutual funds, with similar names and likely run by the same companies. Some are linked to the stock market; some are linked to bonds, among other options. Of the three types, the variable annuity offers the greatest array of investment options.

The choice between which type of annuity is right for you requires a conversation between you and your professional advisor.

Variable Annuity

A variable annuity is a contract that provides fluctuating (variable) rather than fixed returns. The key feature of a variable annuity is that you can control how your premiums are invested by the insurance company. Thus, you decide how much risk you want to take and you also bear the investment risk.

Most variable annuity contracts offer a variety of professionally managed portfolios, called subaccounts or investment options, that invest in stocks, bonds, and money market instruments, as well as balanced investments. Your premiums will be allocated among the subaccounts that you select.

Variable annuities offer fluctuating returns. The return on a variable annuity is based on the performance of the subaccounts that are selected. Any guarantees are contingent on the claims-paying ability of the issuing insurance company. The investment return and principal value of an investment option are not guaranteed. Variable annuity subaccounts fluctuate with changes in market conditions. When a variable annuity is surrendered, the principal may be worth more or less than the original amount invested.

Variable annuities also offer the potential for tax deferral. The taxes on all interest, dividends, and capital gains are deferred until withdrawals are made. Annuity withdrawals are taxed as ordinary income and may be subject to surrender charges plus a 10% federal income tax penalty if made prior to age 59½. Surrender charges may also apply during the contract's early years.

Variable annuities have contract limitations, fees, and charges, which can include mortality and expense risk charges, sales and surrender charges, investment management fees, administrative fees, and charges for optional benefits. Surrender charges may apply during the contract's early years in the event that the contract owner surrenders the annuity. Variable annuities are not guaranteed by the FDIC or any other government agency, nor are they guaranteed or endorsed by any bank or savings association.[xxiii]

Equity Indexed Annuity

In the wake of two stock market crashes in one decade, the Equity indexed annuity (EIA) has become increasingly popular because most (if not all) EIAs protect the initial investment from decline, as long as the rules surrounding the EIA are followed. Usually EIAs have comparatively longer surrender periods than other annuities because of the guarantees. Some EIAs also offer guaranteed income for life; like the variable annuity, this comes at an additional annual cost.

Tax Benefits of Annuities

Annuities accumulate money tax-deferred. As noted above, you can contribute much larger amounts of money into an annuity than you can contribute to an IRA or a Roth IRA or even a 401k. You can also purchase an annuity inside a qualified account; this is called a qualified annuity.

Qualified Annuity: An annuity purchased inside an IRA, Roth IRA or other account qualified with the IRS for a tax deduction.

The initial investment amount inside a non-qualified annuity—that is, any annuity not held inside an IRA, Roth IRA, or other tax-qualified vehicle—is your tax basis. All growth inside the annuity is tax-deferred. When you start taking income, you start the taxation. How you take your income determines how you are taxed.

Withdrawals

If you pull income from the annuity using one of the popular "Guaranteed Income (or Withdrawal) Riders," then you first pull out the growth and are taxed at your income tax rate. After the growth is depleted, you have a zero tax burden on the rest of your withdrawals because it is considered a return of basis. Note that, depending upon the contract, early withdrawals may be subject to a penalty.

Annuitization

If you annuitize, as you do in an immediate annuity, then a portion of every payment is considered a return of basis and is not taxed. A portion of every payment is considered growth and is taxed.

A simple example may help to show the tax advantages of annuitization. William deposits $500,000 in an immediate annuity. The annuity company calculates that 90% of his income is a return of principal and comes back to him every year, for the rest of his life, income-tax free. He will have to pay income tax on the other 10%. If he receives $40,000, his taxable income is only $4,000—a real tax savings!

And Why Not?

What are the shortcomings with annuities?

Surrender Charges and Other Costs

No life insurance or annuity product is free of charges, and sometimes these charges are difficult to find and understand. Costs could include mortality and expense (called M&E), surrender charges, management fees, and charges associated with riders, among others. There could also be penalties for early withdrawals. Find a professional to help you understand the charges completely. You might earn a better rate of return in a product with lower fees, but would you have stayed the course without the guarantees provided by these unique products? For many people, the guarantees are worth the cost. Talk to your professional to be certain that you understand the costs and benefits.

Complicated Products

Annuities are complex products. Many of the investment options, as well as the guarantees, are unique to annuities and thus are not well understood. Even within the financial services industry, great differences in opinion exist about the benefits and shortcomings of the various investments and guarantees. Make sure you and your advisor have a great— not just good— conversation about this so that you truly understand each other. Your advisor should understand you and your needs, and you really need to understand what you are purchasing. Once you understand the details of the product and have all your questions answered, you will be able to make the best choice for your unique financial needs.

Short-term Needs Outweigh Benefits of Time

Deferred annuities are long-term investment strategies, and the benefits grow with time. If you are most concerned with the short-term, then you may not be able to realize the benefits of these investment plans. Instead, look to an immediate annuity or other ideas with short-term stability.

Go Tax Free and Arbitrage an Annuity and Life Insurance

CHAPTER 7

Arbitrage: a risk-free investment opportunity

How This Benefits Me

Arbitrage between a life insurance contract and an annuity is a great plan for folks who have reached "a certain age." This plan generally works better the older you are.

Example

William is 77 years old. He is healthy and plans to live a quality life for as long as he has time on earth. He wants to maximize his income and minimize his taxes. He also wants to leave a legacy for his children. William purchases an immediate annuity guaranteed to make payments to him for life. He then uses a portion of the annuity payment to make life insurance premiums. A large portion of the annuity payment is tax-free, because of a unique annuity benefit. In addition, his children inherit the life insurance death benefit when he dies.

Using an Annuity with Life Insurance and Creating Arbitrage

William has the ability to purchase a life insurance policy with a death benefit of $500,000. He will pay for the annual premiums using a portion of his annuity income stream. The annuity income is largely tax-free. The difference between the income and premium is an arbitrage, or risk-free, investment for him.

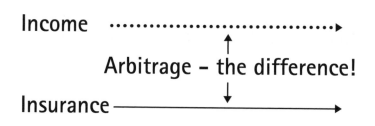

First, William applies for life insurance and finds out how the insurance company will rate him. In so doing, his agent argues for his solid health and good exercise routine. He will likely live a very long time, so his life insurance premiums will be low. His life insurance company has less risk and will collect more premiums from him the longer he lives.

Second, William invests $500,000 with an annuity company. His agent shops various annuity companies to see who will provide the highest income possible for his situation. He wants a life-only annuity, so the annuity company has less risk and less outlay if he dies sooner.

As soon as the first annuity payment arrives, William writes a check to the life insurance company, and he repeats this process once a year for the rest of his life. He will have to pay taxes on a pro-rated portion of his investment. Because of today's low interest rates and because of his age (and comparatively short life expectancy), the income stream is largely tax-free because of the exclusion ratio. His beneficiaries, upon his death, receive a check for $500,000, tax free!

And Why Not?

Why not do this?

Too Young

If you are too young, this will not work. The income is too small. The exact age range for this plan depends upon the companies, interest rates, and the year in which you apply.

Insurance Costs

If you are uninsurable or the insurance is too cost-prohibitive, this plan will not work. Try a trial insurance application before you actually apply just to see if your medical situation is in the ballpark. Your insurance expert should be able to talk with underwriters and give you an idea of your underwriting classification before you submit the full application.

Go Tax Free for a Charity

Absolute: The federal government rewards certain behaviors with tax incentives. We can take advantage of these rewards.

How This Benefits Me

Donating money feels good and aligns your income and assets with a cause you feel passionate about. It creates legacy benefits by removing the asset from your taxable estate. Donations can eliminate taxes on a highly appreciated asset, like a business or a farm. Plus, you get recognition for making a large gift while you are alive, for instance, by endowing a chair at your alma mater.

Example

Bill and Linda worked at large corporations for many years. They believe in saving and not spending more than they earn. Now they have quit the corporate life and would like to save some of their assets from the taxes, passing on their wealth to their children, grandchildren, and church. They enlist the help of an attorney and financial planner and create a charitable remainder trust as well as a wealth replacement trust to accomplish their goals. They enjoy a tax-deductible charitable donation, avoiding taxes on the gains of their investments, and they generate income for both of their lives. They are proud of the gifts they have made to their heirs and their church.

Charitable Trusts

What is a trust?

Even if you think you know the answer to this question, it is very helpful to focus on the fundamentals first. A trust is a legal agreement governing the dispensation of property. A trust has several important parts, each with different legal meanings:

- *Donor, settlor, grantor, trustor:* The person who initially owns the assets and sets the rules for the trust.

- *Trustee:* Different from (and commonly confused with) the donor, a trustee follows the rules of the trust to make sure the assets and income are in order and the taxes are paid. The trustee obeys the rules of the trust and works on behalf of the beneficiary.

- *Beneficiary:* The beneficiary receives some or all of the income and/or assets in the trust. The beneficiary, donor, and trustee are usually not the same person.

- *The trust objective.* The trust objective determines the trust type. In other words, the objective of the trust is the donor's goal, clearly stated, regarding the dispensation of the property. Different types of trusts provide different benefits. A charitable remainder trust is a specific type of trust with an objective of providing income for the donor and future money for a charity.

- *Property:* Trust property may include securities like stocks and bonds, annuities, real estate, businesses, and other real and normal property.

How a Charitable Remainder Trust (CRT) Works

A charitable remainder trust (CRT) is a way to provide income for the beneficiary and a gift for a charity. Additionally, the donor can donate highly appreciated assets because he or she avoids paying taxes on the gains. The donor receives a tax deduction on the present value of the gift to be given to the charity.

History of the CRT

The Tax Reform Act of 1969 made the charitable remainder trust possible, and the tax benefits are governed by IRS Code 664. The money inside the CRT is tax-exempt. The income that comes from the trust is taxable to the income beneficiary. Upon the beneficiary's death, the remainder of the CRT transfers to the charity of the donor's choice.

Rules Regarding the Tax Deduction

The gift made to the irrevocable CRT is a tax deduction in the year of the gift. The size of the tax deduction is determined by the future residual value of the CRT. The tax deduction is not the entire value of the gift made this year. The key factors that go into this calculation include:

- Life expectancy of beneficiary
- Number of beneficiaries (the more beneficiaries, the lower the present value)
- Income rate (the higher the income from the CRT, the

lower the future value)
• Residual value must always be at least 10% of the initial gift

Clearly, this calculation requires expert legal and tax advice. If the income tax deduction cannot be used in the first year, it may be carried forward on the donor's income tax return for up to five years.

Also note that the size of the tax deduction likely has little or no relationship to the actual amount remaining at the end of the trust's term. The charity may receive more than or less than the estimated amount at the beginning of the calculation. There is a possibility that the charity receives nothing from the CRT. Proper management by professionals is critical to avoid the possibility of the CRT value running to zero.

Avoid Capital Gains Tax

Any appreciated asset donated to a CRT is no longer subject to capital gains tax. This is a great way for small business owners and successful investors to transfer highly appreciated assets and not worry about taxes eating up a lot of their value. A CRT is best used for highly appreciated assets, especially if the owner is worried about having to sell the assets and the associated tax ramifications.

Rules Regarding the Income

The donor determines the income withdrawn from the CRT, as well as the duration of that income. Generally speaking, the CRT could last for the life of the beneficiary, or the lives of multiple beneficiaries. In some cases, a CRT is set up to pay for a certain number of years, not to exceed 20. The income can be deferred until later but once it starts, it needs to continue for the duration.

The income must be at least 5% of the account value per year and can be as large as 50% per year. The amount of the income depends upon whether the income stream is a charitable remainder annuity trust (CRAT) or a charitable remainder unitrust (CRUT).

CRAT: Charitable Remainder Annuity Trust. A CRAT pays a fixed dollar amount every year to the beneficiaries. Even though it is called an annuity, a CRAT is not the same as the commercial annuity we discussed earlier.

A CRAT is best for beneficiaries who want to be paid a fixed dollar amount every single year, and it is typically used for older beneficiaries. The CRAT pays a fixed income to the beneficiary regardless of the performance of the underlying investments. For example, a $1 million initial CRAT would pay at least $50,000—5% of the initial account value, as noted above— or more, depending on the donor's wishes. The income continues for the duration of the trust, which is also set by the donor.

CRUT: Charitable Remainder Unitrust. A CRUT pays a fixed percentage, but not a fixed dollar amount, every year.

A CRUT is best for beneficiaries who want inflation protection and are comfortable living with the risk that the income might decline. These are usually younger beneficiaries. The CRUT pays a percentage of the current value of the investment. For example, a $1 million initial investment pays $50,000 the first year. In the second year, the income is 5% of the new account value; thus the income could either shrink or grow. If the CRT value falls to $900,000, then the income is $45,000 in year two. If it grows to $1.1 million by the second year, then the income is $55,000, or 5% of the new account value.

Recover the Gift with a Wealth Replacement Trust (WRT)

One reason folks worry about creating a CRT is that they disinherit their children or other beneficiaries. After all, everything given to the CRT is an irrevocable gift to a charity. To avoid this dilemma, the donor creates a wealth replacement trust (WRT) funded with life insurance on the donor's life. This way, when the last income check comes in upon the death of the donor, the life insurance proceeds pay a lump sum of money that replaces the charitable gift.

The donor is in control of the size of the WRT. The size of the life insurance policy death benefit could be linked to the future value of the CRT, providing a smaller benefit for the family. Or, the life insurance death benefit could be linked to the initial gift—or any other variable, for that matter. The WRT could be a way to leverage the CRT into a nice gift for charity and a much larger gift for the family.

The wealth replacement trust is held outside the donor's estate. This means that the death benefits are not subject to estate tax. Additionally, it means premiums into the WRT are considered gifts and are subject to gifting limits. In 2013, the gift limits are $14,000 per donor. Premiums in excess of that amount count against the donor's lifetime gift tax limits.

An example illustrates it best. Bill and Linda donate $1 million to their CRT and simultaneously create a WRT. Their first-year income from the CRT is $50,000 per year, lasting for 20 years or the length of both of their lives (a CRUT). They use $15,000 per year to pay for a life insurance policy with a $1 million death benefit. Their tax professional estimates that the present value of the gift to their charity is $86,000, so they receive an $86,000 tax deduction in the year they make the gift. Now they have made a meaningful gift to their charity, received recognition from the charity while they are alive, provided an income for themselves, and still provided a $1 million inheritance for their children.

If Bill and Linda choose to invest the entire income of their CRT in the WRT, then they may be able to buy a significantly larger death benefit for their family, creating a larger financial legacy for their heirs.

Held outside the estate, the WRT is not subject to estate taxes upon the donor's death. Any amounts paid into the WRT above the annual gift limits count against the husband and wife lifetime gifting limit. They consult their tax planning advisors throughout the process to make sure this is the best way for them to achieve their goals.

And Why Not?

Why not go tax free for a charity? Well, for starters, it might not work out as planned.

Income Risks

The investments inside the CRT might not produce the same income that you start with if you chose a CRUT, and this could cause stress. The CRT may not generate enough income to fund the WRT life insurance premiums. These are really investment risks, requiring prudence from the trustee and his or her advisors.

Asset Risks

If you choose a CRAT, and enjoy a steady income, the principal might not last, and the income payments may cease before your life ends. And, of course, the charity may or may not get the entire initial planned gift. This too is an investment risk, requiring prudence from the trustee and his or her advisors.

Charitable Deduction

If you just gave $1 million to a charity you would receive a $1 million deduction, compared to a significantly reduced deduction inside the CRT. Sometimes, it makes sense for the purely philanthropically inclined to put their gifts inside a box with bows and ribbons instead of wrapping it a legal trust.

Insurability

To create the wealth replacement trust, the donor must qualify for life insurance. If the donor is uninsurable, then another person could be the insured.

Children

Children may wonder why the money is going to a charity instead of directly to them, straining relationships.

Complexity

Although the plan, once understood, is fairly straightforward, it is not as easy to understand as writing a check to a charitable organization. For some folks, simplicity is in and of itself the best gift. For others, the customization that comes implicitly with a CRT and WRT is energizing and, of course, tax savings and life insurance provide additional leverage.

Go Estate Tax Free in Lifetime Trusts

Absolute: *"Over and over again courts have said that there is nothing sinister in so arranging one's affairs as to keep taxes as low as possible. Everybody does so, rich or poor; and all do right, for nobody owes any public duty to pay more than the law demands: taxes are enforced exactions, not voluntary contributions. To demand more in the name of morals is mere cant."* Commissioner v. Newman, 159 F.2d 848, 851 (2d Cir. 1947) —dissenting opinion, Judge Learned Hand

Absolute: *Estate taxes are mandatory; disinheritance is up to you.*

How This Benefits Me

In 2013, estate taxes affect anyone with more than $5.25 million in assets. Consider ways to keep the assets in the family, tax free. Protect survivors and future generations from creditors, predators, and their own possible bad habits and/or bad relationships.

Example

Michael and Leslie are working professionals in their 50s and have accumulated enough assets over the years that they are within the estate tax range. Their daughter, in her twenties, is single and has some health issues. Their son is married and planning a family. They decide to set up trusts today to protect themselves, knowing that the laws will likely change in the future. They like the flexibility these plans give them. They can accommodate future grandchildren. Additionally, they can protect their daughter in case her health deteriorates and they are not here to help her. They feel confident they can change beneficiaries and their plans at any time and rest easy knowing their affairs are in order.

How Estate Taxes Work

In 1916, the federal government established laws to tax the value of a deceased person's assets and the estate tax was born. All of the deceased person's assets are added together. If the total of the assets is greater than the applicable exclusion amount (below), then that amount is subject to the estate tax rate shown below. If he or she is married, the assets can transfer to the living spouse without incurring estate taxes.

Applicable Exclusion Amount

The applicable exclusion amount is the amount of money that can transfer without an estate tax. For the purposes of this book, we will call this the "exclusion amount." This amount is large enough that most families do not have to worry about the estate tax. The exclusion amount is the key to understanding the entire estate tax system:

Estate Taxes

	Tax %	Exclusion Amount
2007	45	$2 million
2008	45	$2 million
2009	45	$3.5 million
2010	0	N/A
2011	35	$5 million
2012	35	$5.12 million
2013	40	$5.25 million

Source: Internal Revenue Code

As you can see, the exclusion amount and estate tax rate is a moving target. With the continual changes in estate tax law, how can anyone make plans?

We must design our plan based on the rules of the game today. If we do this right, then we can change our plans when the rules change in the future. If our attorneys draft our documents carefully, then our plans can change as the tax law changes. However, there is always a chance that the laws will change in an unexpected manner, requiring a rewrite of our current best-laid plans.

Inheritance Tax

Absolute: Estate tax looks at the deceased person's assets. Inheritance tax looks at the living person's (the beneficiary's) inheritance.

The estate tax looks at a person's overall assets and assesses the tax. An inheritance tax, levied by some states, looks at the recipient. The estate tax treats the inheritance tax as a deduction. Inheritors can take some small satisfaction in that.

Gift Tax

Building on the estate tax, the federal government created the gift tax in 1932 to avoid transfers from a wealthy parent to his or her children while Mom and/or Dad was still alive. Today, the gift tax is tied to the same rate as the estate tax.

Generation Skipping Transfer Tax

In 1976, the federal government created the generation-skipping transfer tax to prevent transfers from grandparent to grandchildren and great-grandchildren skip generations without incurring an estate tax.

How Trusts Help

Trusts help family stewards keep money in the family. To this end, assets are moved out of an individual's ownership and into the ownership of a trust.

A settlor sets rules around how the money may be used in the future by the beneficiaries of the trust. To keep the assets outside a taxable estate, some of these rules persist across all similar trusts. Outside of this similarity, attorneys customize trusts for each individual's unique situation and goals.

Trusts can mitigate estate taxes and protect against creditors, as well as spendthrift beneficiaries and their spouses.

Non-Traditional Relationships

Trusts offer an effective means of transferring assets to folks we love, whether or not this relationship is recognized by the government. Modern families benefit greatly from trusts because, without this type of estate planning, assets transfer according to probate rules. This can mean that money transfers to family members with whom the deceased may not have had a close relationship at all.

Living Trust

A living trust provides a way to organize your assets while you are alive. Your attorney may want you to own most, or all, of your assets in a living trust. One of the key reasons to own a living trust is to make it easy to fund the AB trust, or ABC trusts, described soon.

A living trust does not protect you from estate tax. A living trust does not protect assets from creditors.

A living trust keeps assets out of probate. It keeps your estate private. It also makes it easy to change the beneficiaries for any of your assets because you only have to change them on one document.

Some attorneys prefer to set up multiple living trusts and others prefer a single living trust. Still others prefer not to use living trusts and instead use the last will and testament to implement the advanced estate planning techniques, described next.

AB Trust

One of the most common ways to structure assets to protect against estate taxes is the AB trust. In brief, you could use the exclusion amount and two trusts to eliminate or reduce your estate tax burden.

To the best extent possible, attorneys write the trusts so that either spouse may be the first to die and, if limits to the tax laws change, so can the funding amounts.

Trust B

The AB trust begins with trust B. Upon the death of the settlor, the executor moves as much money as allowed under the exclusion amount into trust B. This money is run through the estate tax system and is now free from any future estate tax burden. The assets may be used according to the rules of the trust set up by the settlor.

Trust B gives the surviving spouse almost as many rights as he or she would have if she had outright ownership of the assets; however, there are some restrictions. The surviving spouse may or may not:

- Be the trustee
- Collect all income from the trust
- Use up to 5% of the principal per year
- Use additional principal for his or her health, education, maintenance, and support (HEMS)
- Direct the distributions of principal from the trust while alive
- Change the beneficiaries of the trust

Trust B gives credit protection; it is not subject to the creditors of the surviving spouse. If the surviving spouse does not need the income or the principal, then this amount of money can grow substantially without an estate tax.

Trust B has several names, including bypass trust, credit shelter trust, and exclusion trust, among others. It is the first trust funded under an AB trust plan and it runs through the estate tax system.

Trust A

Trust A is funded with all of the money that exceeds the exclusion amount. This means that trust A might never be funded if the future exclusion amount is greater than the value of the decedent's estate.

Trust A must be used for the benefit of the spouse. All income from the trust is for his or her benefit. Additionally, the spouse may use the principal for any reason.

Trust B: Because I died first, this trust gets as much money as allowed under the exclusion amount.

Trust A: After I've funded trust B, my spouse gets all the income and assets inside trust A.

The surviving spouse has total control over the assets in trust A and may use them for any reason. The assets in trust A qualify for the "unlimited marital deduction," eliminating estate taxes upon the first death.

Upon the second death, if the assets inside trust A are greater than the future exclusion amount, then the estate owes estate taxes. Life insurance is typically the least expensive way to solve this problem.

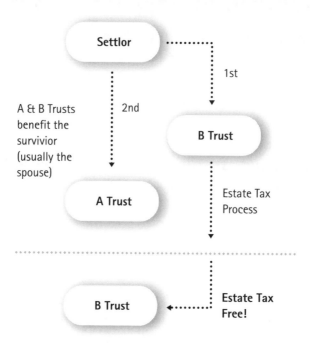

C Trust Planning

Additionally, some attorneys recommend a third trust, called a C trust, when the spouses have different goals from each other regarding the inheritance of their assets. The C trust protects against survivor's creditors. It is more limited than the A or B trusts.

The C trust can go by several names, including marital trust, QTIP Trust, QDot Trust and income and general power of appointment trust. Each has a particular benefit and set of rules.

The C trust is usually a qualified terminable interest in property, or QTIP. This account generates income for the spouse. The assets, upon the first spouse's death, cannot be changed by the survivor, except that he or she can demand that unproductive assets generate more income. The survivor cannot change beneficiaries. They are directed from the grave.

ILIT: Irrevocable Life Insurance Trust

Taxable estates often have another trust that holds a life insurance policy. An irrevocable life insurance trust (ILIT) is outside the estate and has no estate tax burden. The life insurance is usually a permanent policy, called a "second-to-die" policy. It insures two lives and pays upon the second death.

To run the ILIT and assure that no estate taxes are owed, the trustee must follow special rules. The most unique rule, and the most common, is called a Crummey letter, named for a United States Court of Appeals case from 1968 involving the estate of Clifford Crummey.

Crummey Letter

An ILIT trustee must send annual letters to the beneficiaries of the trust, called Crummey letters. The purpose of the Crummey letter is to make sure that the ILIT stays outside the taxable estate.

Every year, premiums are paid into the ILIT. These premiums must count as "present interest gifts" in order for the future proceeds of the life insurance policy to remain estate tax free. Crummey letters are negative consent letters. Recipients do not reply and, by doing so, disclaim their rights to the premium payments in assurance that they will receive an inheritance.

Generation Skipping Trusts

The greatest benefits of trust planning are realized by your children, their children, and future generations. Through lifetime trust planning, you can set up a generation-skipping trust that lasts the lifetime of a beneficiary. It is then passed on to the next generation of beneficiaries, where it once again bypasses estate taxes.

In other words, with a generation-skipping trust, your wealth goes through the estate tax system once and never again.

A few million dollars could grow to hundreds of millions, or billions, and not be subject to the estate tax. Clearly, this is a powerful way to keep money in the family, avoiding the estate tax for generations.

Additionally, trusts provide creditor protection for the beneficiaries. A beneficiary could be the trustee, retaining control as if she had outright ownership of the assets. Trusts are completely customized and the settlor can give the beneficiaries as much, or as little, control over the assets as they wish.

And Why Not?

Not everyone needs advanced estate planning techniques.

I'm Not That Wealthy

If you do not have a taxable estate, and may never have one, then advanced estate planning techniques seem irrelevant. If you do not have enough money to qualify, you might still want to consider estate planning because of the ability to control your assets from the grave. You could protect your children or grandchildren from their own bad habits, or from their spouses, or from creditors.

I Like to Keep it Simple

The simplest course that achieves your goals is often the best course to follow. AB trust planning is widespread and common. Even for folks who practice in the field on a daily basis, we sometimes have to take two steps back and ask ourselves, "Is all this really necessary? Is there an easier way?" Keep asking yourself these questions as you go down the path and you might find other ways to accomplish your goals.

I Didn't Inherit Anything, Why Should They?

Ultimately, either your chosen beneficiaries or Uncle Sam will get the assets you have collected in your lifetime. At minimum, consider creating an exit plan so that your survivors know what you would like to see done with the sum of your hard work. To put your affairs in order is an act of love and respect for your survivors.

Go Tax Free in a 529 Education Savings Plan

Absolute: "If the IRS took 100 taxpayers at random and sent each an incorrect notice that they owed an extra $92.35 in taxes and interest, more than two-thirds would probably just send in a check without investigating further." —G. Guttman

How This Benefits Me

A 529 education savings plan offers state-tax deductible funding, tax-deferred growth, tax-free use of the money for education purposes, and estate-tax free transfer to relatives.

Example

Helen wants to help pay for her grandchildren's college costs. This, of course, is a gift to both her children and her grandchildren. She creates a single 529 plan to benefit all of her nine grandchildren. She could set up nine (or more) plans, but she opts for a single plan to keep it simple. She maximizes her contributions in the first year by putting in five years of contributions. In subsequent years, she contributes the maximum allowable gift amount. If any of the children do not use the money for college, she rests easy knowing she can change the beneficiaries at any time, for any reason. When she passes away, the money can still be used for education for any of Helen's blood relatives. In her own way, she has created an education endowment for her family's benefit.

What is a 529 Plan?

A 529 plan is an investment vehicle that provides tax advantages for the donor as long as the money is used to fund education for the beneficiaries. There are two different types of plans, prepaid and savings plans. The majority of this chapter covers savings plans.

Prepaid Plans

Only a few states still allow existing account-holders to contribute to prepaid plans. Nonetheless, you should know what they are. Prepaid plans limit your student to attending a specific school, usually a large in-state university. Additionally, they limit where and on what items you can spend the money. The biggest benefit of a prepaid plan is that you are able to lock in the tuition rate for that school, regardless of future costs. For many folks, the flexibility of the savings plan outweighs the benefit of the prepaid plan, which is why prepaid plans are becoming largely obsolete.

Savings Plans

Savings plans give owners more flexibility about where the money may be spent and toward what ends. The rest of this chapter covers 529 savings plans.

529 Savings Plan Limits

A 529 savings plan is a vehicle that provides you and your beneficiaries many benefits, as long as the rules are obeyed.

What Can I Spend My 529 Money On?

The 529 savings plan can be used to pay for "qualified higher education expenses." This generally means that if you cannot attend the school without these expenses, then you may use the 529 plan to pay for them. For example, you can spend your money on tuition, books, and room and board. You can spend it on computers, software, and internet access. You cannot pay down your student loans with 529 dollars. You may not spend it on gas, pizza, or video games. 529 plans pay for the cost of attending school, not the cost of traveling to and from the school.

If you have off-campus housing, then you are allowed to use 529 dollars to spend the same amount of money as you would spend on on-campus housing. As a student, there are many other associated costs, including a lock for a locker or a towel for a gym class; for a film student, the cost to attend a required film may be appropriate. The applicability of all of these items becomes a personal preference between you and your tax professional. Keep in mind the rule: the plan pays only for qualified educational expenses.

What Schools May I Attend?

A 529 plan is not just for in-state colleges. In fact, a 529 plan is not just for college. It can be used for an array of educational institutions.

They can be used at public and private institutions. Trade and technical schools apply. Qualifying two-year associate degrees also are appropriate. As a general rule, you can use the 529 money at any post-secondary institution listed in the U.S. Department of Education student financial aid programs. Often, this includes study abroad programs.

Income Tax Benefits

The 529 plan accrues money tax-deferred. As long as the money is used to fund education plans, the money (including the growth) is tax free. Additionally, many states provide state income tax deductions for contributions in their own plans. For example, residents of Colorado who contribute money into a State of Colorado 529 plan reduce their taxable income by the amount of the deduction, saving the tax rate of 4.63%.

In other words, a 529 plan can be a tax-deductible and tax-free investment vehicle, as long as the rules are followed.

Estate Tax Benefits

The 529 plan is NOT included in the estate of the owner. This provides an estate planning opportunity for both recipients and donors. As discussed next, the beneficiaries can be changed. The 529 plan can become part of a grandparent's legacy, transferring from blood generation to blood generation, income-tax and estate-tax free.[xxiv]

Beneficiaries

The owner can change beneficiaries on a 529 plan once per year and for any reason. Unlike some other college savings vehicles, the 529 plan is controlled by the owner, and the beneficiaries have no say in who receives the money, or in when or how much they will receive.

Maximize Contributions

In many state plans, you can contribute more than $300,000 to a 529 plan. Gifting limits usually limit the contributions. In 2013, the per-beneficiary gift limit is $14,000. You can contribute five years of gifts this year, or $70,000. For a married couple, that means you can contribute $140,000 into two 529 plans. The couple could not contribute for the next five years into those plans and must spread the tax deduction over five years. However, they could create a new plan and contribute the same into that plan for another beneficiary.

Tuition Payments Are Not Gifts

Tuition payments are not subject to gifting rules. Thus, grandparents could make payments directly to an institution on behalf of their grandchildren-students, in addition to setting up 529 plans. This important point is sometimes forgotten in college planning.

Other Education Savings Plans

Each of these plans has pros and cons. You may run into one or more of them, and so a brief discussion of each will suffice.

UGMA/UTMA: Uniform Gift/Transfer to Minors Act

An UGMA is taxed at the minor's tax rate. The minor takes control of the asset at age 18 or 21, depending upon the age of majority in the state. The gift tax rules limit the size of the contributions. The assets are also included in the donor's estate. Compared to the 529 plan, the UGMA/UTMA plans are limited.

Coverdell Education Savings Account

Coverdell accounts accumulate money tax deferred. Contributions are limited to $2,000 per year. The beneficiary must use the money on education or give it to another young person for education before they reach age 30 to avoid taxes and penalties. Here is one key advantage: you can spend Coverdell money on elementary or secondary school, something you cannot do in a 529 plan.

And Why Not a 529 Plan?

Reasons why the 529 Savings Plan may not be appropriate include:

Education Only

The benefits are for education only. You cannot use this plan for your own benefit outside of education. This is not a supplemental retirement income plan. There is a 10% penalty for non-qualified withdrawals.

Limited Contributions

Contribution limits make it difficult to transfer sizable amounts of money outside the family's estate or to eliminate significant amounts of income.

Investment Restrictions

Investment options vary from state to state, and some states perform better than others. That being said, the Internet has incredible resources to compare plans and, not surprisingly, investment performance is becoming more equal across the various plans. One IRS-imposed limitation is that you cannot move your assets more than once per year, unless you make a new contribution. With each new contribution, you can make a reallocation.

No Bankruptcy Protection

Most state 529 plans do not exclude the 529 assets from bankruptcy proceedings. Alaska is the notable exception.

Go Tax Free in Municipal Bonds

CHAPTER 11

Absolute: As interest rates go up, bond prices go down.

Absolute: Interest rates are at all-time lows in 2013. On the other hand, bond prices are at all-time highs in 2013.[xxv]

How This Benefits Me

Municipal bonds can potentially offer a tax-free income that is not linked to the stock market.

Example

Bob left his full-time job as a software engineer having accumulated assets and paid off his debts. He now wants to purchase investments that generate a steady, tax-free income for the rest of his life. He understands that interest rates are low today but, as he says, "What can you do?" He is not worried about inflation because he also has a large pool of inflation-fighting investments, including stocks, and a pension that is adequate for his lifestyle. He purchases $1 million in municipal bonds and a municipal bond mutual fund. His annual after-tax income is $45,000 from this portfolio, which suits him just fine.

How Bonds Work

A bond is a promise made by an institution to accept your money and, in return, the institution makes regular payments to you until an agreed upon date when it returns your initial investment. Most bonds make payments, called coupons, every six months.

Bonds are loans. If you loan money to a relative, you expect them to pay it back over a certain period of time. You charge the borrower an interest rate for the convenience of using your money and the inconvenience of not being able to use it. What makes bonds more interesting is that they are bought and sold many times.

An example illustrates this well. A large company, or a municipality, issues a bond and Bob buys it. Bob decides to sell it, for any reason and at any time, to Susie. Susie likely does not pay the same price Bob paid for the bond. Why? Here are the three main reasons. First, Bob has already received several income payments she will not receive. Second, she will wait less (less duration) to receive her principal. Third, interest rates change over time.
Bob has already received several interest payments (coupons) that Sue will not receive. Thus, her total income over the time she holds the bond will be smaller than if she had bought the bond when Bob purchased it.

The duration of the bond defines how long the owner must wait until the bondholder receives the principal. Which would you prefer to have, a bond that pays 5% for five years or a bond that pays 5% for ten years? Stated another way, would you feel safer waiting five years or ten years for your money back? The five year bond is more valuable because it is less risky—a lot could happen over the extra five years.

Think about it this way: the shorter the duration, the lower the risk, the more valuable the bond.

The price also depends upon current interest rates, which fluctuate over time. Susie is willing to pay a fair price for Bob's bond, depending upon what she could expect from another, similar bond. If Susie can get a similar bond that pays a higher interest rate, then the value of Bob's bond is lower than what he paid. If Susie can only find comparable bonds with lower payments, then Bob's bond is comparatively more valuable.

As interest rates go up, bond prices go down. The longer the duration of the bond, the higher the bond holder's risk. These are two fundamental principles regarding bond prices. These absolutes about bond prices bring up a special risk for bond investors at this particular point in time. With historically low interest rates, we are likely looking at interest rate increases in the future. This means that bonds issued today with low rates will likely be worth less in the future, when rates are higher. Talk to your advisor about strategic investment decisions for your situation in today's low interest rate market.

How Municipal Bonds Work

A municipal bond is an agreement with a county, city, school district, special purpose district, public airport or seaport, or other local government organization smaller in size than a state.

Municipal bond income is generally exempt from federal and state taxes. If a municipal bond is issued in your state, then the interest paid from that bond is likely exempt from state income tax. Most municipal bonds are exempt from federal taxes. And, if you have a city tax, and the bond is issued from your local municipality, then it may be exempt from local taxes as well. This is called "triple tax-exempt."

Tax exemption increases the value of a municipal bond. Again, an example works best. If Susie's bond is a tax-exempt municipal bond, she is willing to pay more for that bond. If her combined federal, state and local income tax add up to 40%, then her bond income is worth more than the income from an equivalent taxable bond. This leads to tax-equivalent pricing, where a buyer looks at how much yield it would take a taxable bond to generate the same after-tax income from a municipal bond:

Here is the math:

$$\frac{\text{Yield}}{\text{(1-Tax Rate)}} = \text{Tax equivalent yield}$$

An example illustrates it even better. Let's look at a $1,000 bond (par value), paying 5% per year (rate), with a $25 coupon in January and July. At her 40% tax bracket, Susie would keep 60% of that income, or (.6 x $50) $30 per year. A taxable bond really provides only a 3% yield to her.

On the other hand, a tax-free municipal bond would be worth as much to Susie as a (5%/60%) 8.33% yield taxable bond. If Susie had a taxable bond that paid her $83 per year, she would pay $33 in taxes (40%) and net $50. This is the same as she will get from her tax-exempt $50 bond.

The effect of tax exemption is that municipalities borrow money at lower rates than corporations and other similarly-sized institutions. Municipal bonds pay less than taxable bonds because of the tax benefits.

Thus, municipal bond investors accept a little more default risk and a little lower comparable return, for receiving less tax risk. Municipal bond investors bet that the municipality will make their payments. Each bond has a slightly different personality, as described next.

Types of Municipal Bonds

Municipalities issue several types of municipal bonds.

General obligation bonds are obligations secured by the general operating budget of the issuing municipality. They are secured by the full faith and credit of the issuer's ability to levy taxes. In many cases, they are voter-approved.

Revenue bonds are secured by tolls from roads and bridges, hospitals, subsidized housing, and water and sewage treatment facilities, among other specific projects. Many are issued by special authorities created for that purpose.

Revenue bonds are specific, with specific risk characteristics. General obligation bonds are generally secured by the taxing power of the issuer. For example, if Bob's bond were a toll-road bond, his income is tied to the ability of that toll road to collect tolls. That may or may not be more risky than a bond tied to the general taxing authority of the same municipality.

Quite quickly, you can see that good municipal bond investors have a different personality than some other investors. The best municipal bond investors enjoy details and like research. For others, municipal bond funds may be a better choice.

Municipal Bond Mutual Funds and Exchange-Traded Funds

A municipal bond mutual fund or exchange-traded fund (ETF) offers a way to incorporate municipal bonds into your portfolio without buying individual bonds. The funds are subject to the same inflation, interest-rate, default, and credit risks associated with their underlying bonds. Municipal bond funds and ETFs generally can be bought and redeemed more easily than individual municipal bonds and have no specific maturity date. Both can invest in several different types of municipal bonds, such as general obligation or revenue bonds.

Just like other mutual funds, a municipal bond fund is a collection of municipal bonds that is purchased and professionally managed by an investment company with the capital from a group of investors. The investment company pools your money with money from other investors and pursues the objectives stated in the mutual fund prospectus.

ETFs are unique in that they combine the diversification of a mutual fund with the flexibility of a stock. Unlike mutual funds, net asset values for ETFs are not calculated each day. Instead, their prices may fluctuate throughout the day based on demand in the open market. ETFs may trade at a discount to their net asset value and are subject to the market fluctuations of their underlying investments.

Although the value of a municipal bond ETF comes from the worth of the underlying assets, shares may trade at a "premium" or a "discount." ETF shares are sold on stock exchanges and can be bought or sold at any time during the day. The underlying assets of the fund are not affected by market trading.

Like mutual funds, ETFs have expense ratios, although they may be lower than those of an average mutual fund. Unlike mutual funds, ETFs have a commission fee. Commissions are involved because ETFs are traded like stocks.

In addition to helping diversify a portfolio, a municipal bond fund or ETF can be used to help generate an income stream that is potentially free from federal and/or state taxation. In some states, investors have to pay income tax if they buy shares of a municipal bond fund that invests in bonds issued by other states. Although some municipal bonds in a fund may not be subject to ordinary income tax, they may be subject to federal or state alternative minimum taxes (AMTs). If a tax-exempt bond fund is sold for a profit, investors could incur capital gains taxes.

You can redeem your municipal bond fund shares at any time for their current market value. The value of the shares is determined daily, based on the total value of the fund divided by the number of shares purchased. The return and principal value of municipal bond fund shares fluctuate with market conditions. Shares, when redeemed, may be worth more or less than their original cost.

Purchasing shares in a mutual fund or ETF can give you access to a diversified portfolio, often without having to spend a large chunk of money and time deciding which types of individual bonds to purchase on your own. Diversification is a method to help manage investment risk, but it does not guarantee against loss.[xxvi]

Odd Lots and Spreads

Unlike individual bonds, which may be difficult to sell at an appealing price, the municipal bond fund is valued daily and an owner in the fund receives that net asset value (NAV). Individual bonds have a much larger spread between the price a buyer is willing to pay and the price a seller is willing to sell.

Take, for example, Bob and Susie. It might be hard for Bob to find Susie, or for Susie to find Bob. So, Bob lists his bond on the market and must pay for the brokerage service. Bob bought just the right amount of bonds for his portfolio, not the right amount for Susie's portfolio. Any amount of bonds other than 100 units is called an "odd lot," and the price decreases for odd lots. Municipal bond funds solve that "odd lot" and spread problem.

Diversification

Municipal bond funds are often issued state-by-state, providing the same triple-tax exemption of the individual issue. This provides advantages and disadvantages for investors. State-specific bond funds are usually smaller in size than the general municipal bond funds, which means the prices could vary more and the diversification is less. Unless an investor makes a lucky investment pick, an investor is likely to be safer with greater diversification. A bond fund has greater diversification than any individual investor in that bond fund.

Municipal bond fund diversification is a key advantage over individual issues in most cases. Although municipal default is rare, defaults have happened and bond owners have lost money. Owning multiple bonds significantly reduces the default risk of any single issuer.

Expense Ratios

Municipal bond funds have fees called an expense ratio that reduce the net return to the investor. Balance the rewards of diversification and professional management with the risks of single issue ownership when choosing whether to invest directly in municipal bonds or in a municipal bond fund. When looking at a single issue, we often err on the side of assuming we know more than we do about risks. We say, "I know that toll road! It's always full. What a great investment." But we do not read about or understand everything that could affect the payments from that road.

On the other hand, issuer default is rare and the owner of a single bond will put more money in her pocket than the owner of the same bond, held with hundreds of others, in a municipal bond fund. Talk with your advisor about the most appropriate choice for your situation, whether it is bond fund or a group of odd lot single issue bonds.

And Why Not?

Why not go tax free in municipal bonds? Here are several reasons.

Interest Rates Are Low

Today's interest rates are at all-time lows. Corporations, mortgages, and bank loans are all very low today. Rates on municipal bonds are even lower because of the tax benefits.

The rates of return for municipal bonds may not be high enough for you to be able to invest and meet your goals.

Rates Rise, Prices Decline

Remember the absolutes: as interest rates rise, bond prices decline. Rates are at all-time lows. And, something that is at the bottom has only one way to go: up. If you purchase a single bond, consider carefully whether you can hold it for the duration because if rates rise, the bond price will decline. The longer the duration, the more the price will decline. If you can hold the bond until it matures, then you will receive your principal (regardless of interest rates).

Liquidity is Important

Liquidity is a benefit. You may want to be able to sell your bond fund if rates rise, and so will everyone else. You will be doubly hurt if you have a single issue, both with the "odd lot" premium price plus the comparably low coupon of your bond. You may want to sell for personal reasons, to fund a medical emergency, vehicle, vacation, or other large expense. In this scenario, bond funds may look timelier today.

Locking It In

A bond holder who can stay the course can lock in an income stream for the duration of her life. This is appealing in a non-inflationary world. However, we do not know what future rates of inflation will be. Every year we live, almost everything we buy gets more and more expensive. Locking in a fixed income in a rising cost world is a long-term recipe for gradual decline.

Go Tax Free and Own Stocks

CHAPTER 12

Absolute: Be an owner not a loaner; owners make more money.

Absolute: Like Cinderella's slipper, an investment portfolio is custom fit for one person.

How This Benefits Me

Stocks are the world's highest long-term returning asset class. Stocks offer tax-deferral on growth. Dividends currently exceed the income from US Treasuries.[xxvii]

Example

Andrew started investing at a very early age with companies he recognized, such as Disney, Coke, and others. He never sold those initial stocks and just watched them grow, reinvesting the dividends, riding through recessions and enjoying stock splits and other corporate events. Now that he has left his full-time job, Andrew purchases a pool of stocks with the help of his advisor. He purchases a diverse array of equities, large and small, global and local, in a number of different businesses. He will defer the taxes on the growth by not selling the stocks. Upon death, his children will inherit a step-up-in-basis, and will be able to sell Andrew's stocks and purchase a portfolio that is right for them.

How Stocks Work

Stocks are units of ownership in a corporation. Unlike bond investors who are loaners, stock investors are owners. The fundamental value of the stock is determined by the company's assets, income, and the company's likely future income stream and growth.

Stock investments are fractional ownership units. While a small business owner owns 100% of his or her company, a stockholder might own .001% of a publicly-traded company, with the other 99.999% owned by thousands of other individuals. Each person has a vote with a weight equal to their percentage ownership.

Two things determine a stock investor's returns: income and growth.

A stock's income is called a dividend. The technical word for growth is capital appreciation. Each is discussed next.

Dividends are cash distributions of profits. They are paid to stock owners, usually quarterly. The dividend can be used by the stock owner in any way she chooses. She may spend it, reinvest it in the stock, or put it back into her portfolio to reinvest in a pool of other investments, which may include other stocks.

Capital appreciation is the growth of the stock price over time. Prices of publicly-traded companies may trade up or down at any given point in time, due to factors described later in this chapter. Fundamentally, however, the value of a company is determined by the Return on Investment (ROI) that the investor expects to receive. All things being equal, if the expected return increases, so does the price.

Dividends and capital appreciation combine to enable stock investors to achieve rates of return that have historically exceeded any other asset class over long stretches of time. Stocks are also subject to price declines that can be dramatic. An individual stock's price can drop all the way to zero. This risk, as with others, can potentially be mitigated by a properly-diversified portfolio.

Initial Public Offering

The private owners of a company enlist the services of a broker to take the company public in an initial public offering (IPO). After setting a price based off the fundamental value, the owner's shares are offered to the public to purchase. The owner keeps the proceeds minus the costs of the investment banking process. From this point forward, the value of the company is determined not just by the cash flows, profitability, growth projections, and other fundamental information. It is also determined by that stock's relationship with other publicly-traded stocks.

The benefits to the private company owner are many. First, the owner receives a nice windfall from the IPO when the public pays for ownership. Second, publicly-traded companies generally have more access to additional money through capital markets than private companies. Third, they have the ability to grow with the market. In a rapidly rising market, the stock price may grow faster than the fundamental price warrants. Fourth, the owners have liquidity and can exit the business faster. These and other benefits of owning publicly-traded companies have led to the birth of one of the greatest wealth creation vehicles in history.

Emily's Technologies, a Story

Let's look at an illustration. Emily's Technologies is a successful publicly-traded stock: EMLY. The company continues to make money through an economic downturn and, in fact, increases its dividend payout. Had the company remained privately-owned, it might have increased in value to its owners. In a publicly-traded stock, this might not be the case. During this downturn, no stocks are immune from a sell-off, and EMLY declines in value.

Stock market downturns are not the only time when a publicly-traded company may not be fairly valued, at least according to its owners. EMLY may face a situation where it is growing, increasing dividends, and otherwise performing for its owners. Yet another company makes even more money than EMLY does, so its price increases quickly and EMLY's price may even decline. On a relative basis, EMLY is not as attractive to investors who want to maximize their returns.

In both cases, the intrinsic value of Emily's Technologies is separated from the publicly-traded price. The value of the company is higher than the price. Under-valued companies present potential opportunities to investors.

Other situations arise where prices are disassociated from value. In fact, companies' share prices are sometimes over-valued, as during the end of the 1990s dot-com bubble. The stock market always corrects. Think about it as a melting pot of the best thinking in the world about the best ways to employ our money to get the best relative returns.

Tax Advantages of Stocks

Stocks are taxed in two ways: short-term and long-term. Building on a recurring theme in this book, long-term thinking is well rewarded.

Short-term gains are taxed at the owner's marginal income tax rate. In other words, dividends and stocks held less than one year incur gains that are taxed at the owner's marginal income tax rate.

Long-term capital gains are taxed at the long-term capital gains rate. Stocks held more than one year, or 365 days, are taxed at the long-term rate when they are sold.

Stocks held and never sold receive a step up in basis upon the owner's death. This means the children, or other beneficiaries, can sell that stock with a zero income-tax burden. They can sell the stocks with no long-term capital gains tax due.

An example illustrates the potential benefits of owning stocks. Andrew owns $1 million of various stocks whose dividends total $35,000 per year. He is taxed at his marginal income tax on the dividends, but he is able to use the money any way he likes. Every year, on average, companies increase their dividends by a rate that exceeds inflation. Over long periods of time, his stocks increase in value at a rate that significantly outpaces inflation.

Stock Market Rates of Return

Over long periods of time, no other asset class outpaces stocks for total return. Dividends and capital appreciation together account for a total return that, on average, has been 9.5% over the last century. [xxviii] Bonds as a category, including all the various flavors, have averaged 4.9% per year.[xxix] Average inflation is 3.3%.[xxx]

What is amazing about stocks and bonds is that at the time of this writing, stocks pay a higher income than United States Treasuries.[xxvii] In other words, an investor can potentially receive the benefits of the best average long-term capital appreciation rates, as well as an income that is larger than he or she could expect from bonds.

Choice and Control

Stocks provide greater choice and control over income than many other investment vehicles. Want more income? Choose a higher dividend stock. Don't need income? Choose a stock with a zero dividend.

Stocks are among the most liquid of investment classes. They are marketable, and trading costs can be low. Large companies often trade with a penny's difference between the buyer's bid and seller's asking price. They are efficient. United States stocks can be seen as the envy of the world for the choice and control they provide their owners.

And Why Not Stocks?

Why not invest in stocks? Here are several reasons.

I Don't Want to Lose My Money

The number one objection to owning stocks is not the promise of capital appreciation but the threat of capital obliteration.

Bad news sells advertisements, and we hear bad news more often than we hear good news. Further, we feel pain in the limbic brain and remember it with deep, ancestral neurons that cause "fight or flight" responses that stick with us for years.

We often have to look for good news. Good investment returns trigger cerebral brain neurons that do not cause an emotional response even remotely close to an equivalent financial loss.[xxxi] We often rationalize our gains and internalize our pains. We measure pain on the Richter scale and gains on a micrometer. Stocks are historically the best returning long-term asset class.[xxix] The price we pay for those excess returns is short-term volatility, and short-term volatility can be both extreme and extremely painful.

Think Long-Term

Long-term thinking creates more wealth than short-term thinking. The problem is that long-term thinking almost always has an associated short-term cost.

All stocks are long-term investments or they are no investment at all. All ownership is ultimately an investment of love and heart and not just a financial endeavor. Stock prices will fluctuate due to factors completely outside of the owner's control, and short-term stock pickers will likely be punished for short-term thinking.

To own stocks, an investor must plan to own them for the long haul. This does not mean, of course, that you cannot or should not sell one poorly performing company for another better investment. Rational long-term behavior is well rewarded in stocks. Rational long-term behavior tells us that the best returning investments are the ones that scare away short-term thinkers and, honestly, profits at their expense.

I Need Income

Folks who need income today may not be comfortable with the risks associated with stocks. Dividend paying stocks provide income, usually quarterly, that can compete with bonds. However, stock prices fluctuate much more dramatically than bonds, and watching these price fluctuations over the short haul can be a recipe for unnecessary stress.

CHAPTER 13

Go Tax Free and Own Real Estate

Absolute: Tax incentives increase real estate values.

Absolute: The 2008 financial crisis was in no small part a result of a real estate bubble, which was in no small part due to real estate tax advantages.

How This Benefits Me

Tax-deductible mortgage interest payments, depreciation, and expenses, among others things, help the net return for real estate owners. Real estate, over the long haul, can appreciate. Investment real estate can potentially provide regular income.

Example

Selena and David purchased real estate over their lives and enter their retirement years with a steady income. Some of it is not-taxable, and the growth on their investments accumulates tax deferred. If they sell one of their properties, they can roll the proceeds tax free into another real estate investment. As they age, they want to reduce the stress and maintenance associated with owning real estate, so they look at consolidating their properties into a larger, professionally-managed investment property.

How Real Estate Works

Owning your own home provides financial and other benefits, including pride and security. Owning a vacation home is a dream shared by many Americans, and can provide freedom, control, and increased quality of life.

Investment real estate works on an entirely different level, providing income and possible appreciation. As an investment, two fundamental principles work to the real estate owner's long-term advantage:

Absolute: Only so much real estate exists.

Absolute: Human population increases over time.

All else remaining equal, real estate grows in value as time passes simply because it is a finite resource with an ever-increasing demand called population growth. However, populations do not grow equally in all areas, and real estate is not scarce in all areas.

All types of real estate enjoy tax advantages. Savvy real estate investors maintain choice and control over their income and their taxes, choosing when and how much they want to pay in taxes.

How Real Estate is Taxed

A primary residence has tax advantages for the owner. The property appreciates tax-deferred. Upon the sale, both a husband and a wife can avoid taxes on $250,000 of gains (each).[xxxii] While they are living in the property, the mortgage interest is tax deductible. Records of improvements, repairs, and maintenance should be organized and used to increase the tax basis, and to reduce the gains, for the date of the future sale.

A second home, or vacation home, is taxed the same way as the primary residence. A total of $1 million dollars in loan value may be deductible for the primary and secondary residence.[xxxiii] Loan values in excess of these amounts are not deductible. Vacation homes cannot be rented more than ten days per year or the income becomes taxable.

Investment real estate is taxed differently. The property owner enjoys tax-deferred appreciation, but upon the sale, the gains are taxed as capital gains. If the property is held more than 365 days, it is taxed at the (always lower) long-term capital gains rate. If the property is a "fix and flip" or held less than a year, it is taxed at the (always higher) short-term capital gains rate. Real estate agents and other real estate professionals are taxed differently. In many cases, they are judged to be doing every real estate transaction as part of their business. Thus, they pay income taxes at the marginal rates and they get full business deductions.

Interest on investment real estate mortgages is tax-deductible in the year it is incurred. All expenses incurred for maintenance, improvements, property management, and other associated costs are deductible, but particular costs may not count as an expense in the year the cost is incurred. Again, keep good records and consult with your advisor to maximize your benefits.

Depreciation and Other Deductions

Real estate depreciates on a tax return, even if the value of the real estate appreciates in value on the balance sheet. Real estate owners should maintain records of repairs and maintenance costs to potentially include them in that year's itemized tax return to mitigate their tax burdens. Various real estate assets depreciate at different rates, and some items can be expensed in a single year.

Depreciation: Any improvement you make to real estate gets worn down over time. The tax breaks taken over time are called depreciation.

Expense: An improvement whose entire cost applies in the year of the purchase as a deduction against income on the tax return.

Working with a tax preparer, CPA, or enrolled agent who is an expert in real estate taxation is a key to success. Maximizing deductions is an easy concept to understand in theory, but it can be much more complicated in practice.

Real Estate in an IRA or Roth IRA

You can purchase real estate inside an IRA or a Roth IRA and obtain the tax advantages of either one of these vehicles, instead of the tax advantages of real estate itself. In other words, the rules for the IRA or Roth IRA override the rules associated with real estate.

Caveat: Many people purchase real estate inside their IRAs without understanding all of the shortcomings. Buyer beware! Do your homework.

The IRA or Roth IRA must run the investment real estate business entirely on its own. You cannot accept income from or make payments on behalf of your IRA's real estate investment. All expenses for the property must be made with money inside the IRA. If there is a loan on the real estate, all payments must come from the IRA account. Property maintenance, improvements, attorney fees, and everything else must come from the IRA.

Some people have run into trouble because their IRA accounts ran out of money to maintain their property, or they just did not understand how serious the wall between IRA and non-IRA money is. Because of the complications surrounding self-directed real estate IRAs, certain companies have grown to become specialized custodians. They are a source of advice for how to manage the accounts.

Real estate owned in an IRA may cause unrelated business income tax (UBIT), which may mean that some of the income from the real estate itself becomes taxable to the IRA owner in the year it is incurred. UBIT is usually caused by mortgage(s) on the IRA-owned real estate, and a good way to avoid it is to avoid debt. UBIT gets complicated quickly, and any IRA owner considering purchasing real estate inside his or her IRA should consult a tax expert with specific experience calculating these costs and, if possible, running the real estate business appropriately to reduce or eliminate UBIT.

1031 Exchange

The IRS recaptures many of the tax advantages of real estate, upon the sale. Depreciation is recaptured at 25% and gains are (usually) captured at the long-term capital gains rate.[xxxiv] To avoid these tax costs, which can sometimes wipe out the investment gains, investors can follow the rules of an IRS code called a 1031 tax-free exchange.

First, the seller must hire a qualified intermediary. In a 1031 exchange, the seller never touches the buyer's money. Instead, the buyer's money transfers to a qualified intermediary who custodies the money until the seller finds a suitable, like-kind investment to purchase. A like-kind investment is usually another real estate property but it can be a royalty interest in an oil or natural gas-producing real property. Be sure to consult with a professional who has experience with 1031 rules before entering into a contract.

Certain rules surround how quickly the seller must identify a new property and then move the money into that property, and violations of these rules cause the transaction to be taxable. Furthermore, the debt to equity ratio of the property sold and the property purchased should be very close in proportion. An increase in debt is not (immediately) a problem, but a reduction in debt is a taxable event called "boot."

The 1031 exchange is a tax-deferral plan. It does not eliminate taxes, it defers taxes. The basis of the original property carries into the future properties and, upon the dissolution of this plan, the IRS recaptures depreciation and gains. The beneficiary of an owner who died with low basis, highly tax-deferred real estate properties receives a step-up in basis to the value upon the owner's death.

And Why Not?

Real estate investments are not for everyone. Reasons include:

Real Estate is Work

Real estate investors wear many hats. They are buyers, sellers, negotiators, property managers, shoppers, hagglers, salespeople, financial controllers, and tax planners. If they are not able to do all these things themselves, they must hire out these roles and then, at minimum, be managers of their experts. Tenants leave, and sometimes they leave badly. The threat of a lawsuit is common and, for the large real estate investor, likely ongoing. Real estate is a highly transactional business. The only thing the person on the other side of the table really wants may be the money in your pocket. This is not a path for the faint at heart or naive.

Real Estate is Risky

Real estate does not always rise in value. As many people discovered during the 2008 financial crisis, real estate also declines in value. The faster it rises in value, the faster it may decline. Real estate often gives us a sense that we know more than we really know, and we feel more confident than perhaps we should. We might get a false sense of security thinking that our investments are worth more than they are simply because they are priced and sold on a market that is not as liquid or as readily apparent as other investments.

Real Estate is Complicated

Numerous tax advantages associated with real estate also attract schemers and dreamers who sometimes make mistakes, and drag along unsuspecting investors with them. Tax schedules, expenses, amortization, and depreciation are but the tip of the iceberg when it comes to looking at an investment in real estate. For folks who already live complicated lives, or who run complicated businesses, real estate can become an expensive distraction. For others looking for something to do, and who naturally enjoy the arena, it can potentially be financially rewarding.

Real Estate is Easy to Enter and Hard to Exit

Real estate is easy to enter and may be hard to exit. Later in life, you may not want to be a landlord. Many of our clients come to us looking for ways to exit real estate and/ or simplify and consolidate their investments—including their properties—to have less hassle and stress. The tax consequences can be high when you sell later. You may find yourself in a trap where taxes are driving your investment decisions. This leads the investor to buy more real estate to defer the tax consequences even longer—a vicious cycle for someone who wants out. As investors get older, real estate investments tend to be more complicated, are seen as more work, and may be less aligned with their investment goals.

Go Tax Free and Own Your Own Business

CHAPTER 14

Absolute: He who owns the gold makes the rules.

Absolute: Losses on tax returns are not necessarily losses on income statements.

Absolute: "I'm proud to be paying taxes in the United States. The only thing is—I could be just as proud for half the money." Arthur Godfrey

If you own a business, congratulations! What can you do to take advantage of tax and investment planning ideas already out there?

How This Benefits Me

The self-employed and other business owners have more choice and control over their taxation and income than anyone else. Making the leap is both scary and easier than you might think.

Example

Ross just quit his job and hired on as a contract employee. After 25 years, Ross became an expert at his particular technological field. He never planned for this to happen, he just put his head down and did an excellent job for all the companies he worked for, for many years, and now he knows as much about his area of expertise as anyone in the country. His wife, Sharon, has a regular job with regular benefits. Although she is not in love with the pay, she likes the company and the people in it. Their kids are raised and out of the house. Now the two of them are ready to focus on themselves, maximizing their assets so they can enjoy a retirement income, pursuing their passions of golf and sailing.

Ross and Sharon decide they are going to quit their jobs and start a contracting business. He is able to deduct all sorts of things that he was already spending money on, and he now has more choice and control over how much taxes they pay and when. Additionally, by moving to a contractor status, his former employer increased his pay because they saved money on the benefits package they no longer have to provide. Ross and Sharon can take a month-long sailing trip through the Caribbean, if they choose. They can finally travel to Scotland and play a round at St. Andrews, and other courses as well. Sharon and Ross feel more financial control and they feel satisfaction in many other areas of their life.

Becoming a Business Owner

Making the leap to business owner is daunting, exciting, and, like many of these ideas, not appropriate for everyone. It is not appropriate to become a business owner simply to obtain more choice and control over your tax situation. The risks associated with becoming a business owner are high and must make economic sense before tax consequences are considered.

As a business owner, your tax situation will be (purposefully) more complicated than it was when you filed only a W2 tax return. You will start to itemize and likely you will start to wonder, is this purchase a tax-deductible expense? You may start having dreams about other business ideas before your original ideas have had time to mature.

Fortunately, the Internet provides a wealth of information about starting and running your own business. Groups of business owners have sprung up all around the country where owners of non-competing businesses share best practices and help push each other forward. You don't need to be brilliant, but you do need to be honest and hard-working to make your own business work, and there is no guarantee that you will make more money than you did as an employee. In fact, you may make less money and take on significantly more risk.

Your Niche

In our example above, Ross has a very specific niche for his business. Originally, it is his prior employer. Both sides win because when he becomes a contractor, Ross gets a higher income, with more choice and control over his hours and his taxes.His employer wins, because Ross the contractor no longer receives the expensive benefits package that Ross the employee received.

The more specific your niche, the more lucrative your business may be. The Ross Consulting LLC business benefits from his expertise as one of the very best in the world at just one thing. Now that he is a consultant, the ways in which he delivers "just one thing" could expand infinitely. He could become a speaker, a trainer, a website owner, a subject-matter expert for the court. He may be able to work for some of his former competitors, depending upon non-compete restrictions and marketplace dynamics. What often happens with business owners is they see more opportunity than they have time, and one of their most difficult decisions is how to focus on the most rewarding, simple things that, at first blush, may seem like the least interesting things to do.

As a business owner, in addition to doing the work that "pays the bills," Ross, at least initially, starts learning and doing other work, like answering the phones, paying bills, invoicing, doing the books, managing inventory, finding new business, and the myriad other tasks that might require an entire department in a larger, established business.

Bookkeeping

One of the least rewarding parts of owning a business can be the business of the business, bookkeeping. Often, a start-up consultant like Ross will do it himself and/or ask his wife, Sharon, to help. It's a good start and there are many, many resources out there to help make the do-it-yourselfer successful. Consider hiring an expert who specializes in one-person consultant firms to help with tax preparation, bookkeeping and all the business of running a business.

Small business development centers at local Chambers of Commerce can be a resource. Additionally, new business owners should look to other business owners for advice, and in the pursuit, find associations that can transform the way we think about our work.

Benjamin Franklin once attributed all of his success to his "Leather Apron Club" of business owner friends who met monthly and provided expert advice to each other. Consider an advisory board part of your checklist if you want to get serious about your business.

Choice and Control

Business owners pay in complexity for the benefits of choice and control. Take Ross Consultants, for example. He forms an LLC, and he could have selected one of many other ways to run his business.

Tax Structures

A business owner must have at least a fundamental understanding of legal structures of ownership to make a good decision for his or her business. Here are the most popular ways for the self-employed, start-ups, and other entrepreneurs to structure a new business.

LLC

The LLC is a Legal Liability Company. LLC owners enjoy minimal legal costs, while achieving protection from legal creditors. Lawsuits against the LLC do not attach to the personal assets of the LLC owners. Seek legal advice to understand the rules associated with making sure that the legal walls are not violated and that your personal assets do not become part of the LLC. The LLC owners can choose to be taxed as a partnership (if more than one owner), a C corporation, or a Sub S corporation.

Partnership

Taxes for a partnership are zero, and all gains or losses are passed through to the individual tax returns of the owners.

Corporation

A corporation, often called a "C corp," is owned by stockholders and is the most common way for large companies to do business in America. The corporation is taxed as its own entity and enjoys the strongest legal protections of any of the structures of business; arguably the strongest protections of any entity in the world. Corporations can, and do, go bankrupt without any of the other assets of their owners being affected. Owners of corporations are taxed twice—once at the corporate level and once at the personal level.

Sub S Corporation

The Sub S corporation is a popular way to own a small business. The Sub S corporation is a pass-through entity, avoiding the double taxation of the C corporation.
One of the advantages of a Sub S corporation versus the partnership or C corporation is that Sub S corporation owners have more choice and control over FICA taxes, described later in this chapter.

The choice between a Sub S corporation and LLC is often a personal preference for many new business owners. At any time, either a Sub S corporation or an LLC can become a C corporation. However, the choice to move back from C corporation to a Sub S corporation is generally a bad one. It is typically best to start with the Sub S corporation and wait until it is necessary to choose C corporation status.

FICA, FUTA, and Other Tax Acronyms

Absolute: The government always gets paid. Business owners have more choice and control over how and when.

Starting with the absolutes, we will look at how and why business owners achieve tax choice and control and pay for these benefits with more complexity. First, look at several important definitions:

- FICA: the Federally Insured Contributions Act, which means Social Security and Medicare taxes.

- Payroll taxes include income tax and FICA. They are paid with every paycheck by employees.
- Social Security is "OASDI: Old Age, Survivors and Disability Insurance." This tax affects the first $113,700 of income earned in year 2013. Employers pay 6.2% and employees pay 6.2%. [xxxv]
- Medicare Tax is 2.9%. Employers pay half, and employees pay half. This affects all income; it does NOT have a cap like OASDI. [xxxv]

Thus, the self-employed see 15.3% of their income disappear before they even see their income tax. Employees, on the other hand, see 7.65% withheld, and do not directly see the remaining percentage that the employer pays on their behalf.

Income tax is a progressive tax that grows from between 10% to 39.6% in 2013, as discussed in chapter two. Additionally, employers pay another tax called the Federal Unemployed Tax Act (FUTA) to pay for the unemployed. Employers pay approximately 0.8% on the first $7,000 of wages earned for their employees. Certain types of labor are exempt. A self-employed person does not pay FUTA unless and until he or she hires employees.

Sub S Corporation Tax Advantage

Let's take a closer look at the business strategy of Ross Consultants. Ross earns $200,000, and he takes it all as salary. The first $113,700 is taxed at 15.3%, and the remainder is taxed at 2.9% for Medicare. His FICA tax burden is $19,898.80.

Instead of taking it as a salary, Ross wants to take all $200,000 as a distribution. A distribution saves him from paying FICA of nearly $20,000! However, he cannot take it all as a distribution—this is an abusive tax practice.

Ross must pay himself a fair and reasonable salary and then he may take the rest as a distribution. In Ross's case, he may have trouble validating an extremely low salary, in spite of his best tax planning ideas, because he has a history of a high salary as an employee doing essentially the same work. He will consult with his tax expert and make a choice that follows IRS guidelines and is right for his situation.

Don't Ruin Your Social Security

On the one hand, saving thousands of dollars a year in FICA tax might benefit small business owners. On the other hand, the money that business owners do not pay into FICA is a fraction of the money they will not receive in Social Security retirement benefits later in life.

Every year, the exact Social Security payments change, but round numbers illustrate the concept. Today, by not paying FICA, a business owner may save thousands of dollars. Today, the maximum Social Security payment is over $30,000 per year, or a large multiple of the likely annual savings.

Additionally, Social Security payments are guaranteed to grow. In a low interest rate environment, give careful thought before you disinherit yourself.

Absolute: If you (or your spouse) do not accrue Social Security credits, then you will not receive Social Security income.

Sub S Corporation Election Saves the FICA Tax

Social Security benefits depend upon the credits paid into the system. Medicare benefits do not. So why pay more than you must into Medicare?

If your overall financial plan includes receiving Social Security income, then you may be comfortable contributing to the Social Security system. You (and/or your spouse) have to pay into Social Security to get your Social Security income. At least you can see a trade-off.

Medicare is a different story. You do not have to pay into the Medicare system to get Medicare benefits. You are forced to contribute 2.9% to Medicare whether you want to or not. If you could avoid paying that tax, you may be inclined to do so.

Absolute: Given current law, you will receive Medicare benefits regardless of whether you choose to take a salary or a distribution.

This thinking leads to an interesting conclusion. Short-term tax planning with a Sub S corporation saves different amounts for different business owners, depending upon how profitable they are. For business owners with profits less than the Social Security maximum taxable income limit ($113,700 in 2013), the additional savings come at the expense of tens of thousands of dollars a year in future Social Security income. For owners of highly profitable businesses, the additional savings is 2.9%.

Instead of maximizing tax savings, you may want to maximize Social Security for both spouses. If you run both spouses through payroll, then both maximize Social Security income benefits. Let's look at a few examples of the unique planning opportunities a Sub S corporation tax election offers the business owner.

Everyone benefits from having more choice and control over both short-term income tax savings and long-term income benefits.

Example 1: Maximize Ross' Social Security

Ross has a self-employed income of $200,000. He chooses to pay himself a salary of $113,700 and take the rest as a distribution, saving $2,502.70 (2.9% x $86,300) in FICA Tax. This is a unique plan for companies taxed as Sub S corporations, and he saves several thousand dollars a year.

Example 2: Minimize Ross's Salary

If Ross chose to pay himself $50,000, then he would save the FICA taxes on the other $150,000. This benefit of the Sub S Corporation is tempting: $50,000 x 15.3% is $7,650 in payroll tax. The savings are substantial at $12,248.90. However, Ross may end up making himself liable for an audit because his salary is too low. He can be at the low end of a range, but the IRS does look at a salary range, so he should be careful about what is justifiable.

Example 3: Employ Sharon, Maximize Future Social Security

Ross may want to employ Sharon for about $80,000. Then she pays both Social Security taxes and Medicare taxes. This way, when she gets to retirement, she also gets to claim her own Social Security income. While both of them are alive, they can receive two checks instead of one check during retirement.

This plan costs $29,818.80 per year in total taxes, or $9,920 more per year than Example 1(maximizing only Ross's Social Security Income.) They would follow this plan if they want to take care of their future selves and maximize their future Social Security income at the expense of extra money today.

Short-term tax savings may have long-term costs.

Short-term tax savings may have long-term income costs for Sharon and Ross, depending upon how long both of them live. They have a business that profits $200,000. But how long will it last? Will it grow? Is there a chance it could disappear? Will it be easier to pay taxes today and get more Social Security income later? Or, are they confident in their business and prefer to maximize their retirement plans without the assistance of Uncle Sam? Their long-term financial plans should determine their short-term course of action.

Example 4: $1 Million in Profits

Let's now assume that Ross and Sharon's business has much larger profits. Here, the Sub S corporation election makes sense because it saves on the large distributions above the owner's salaries. A business with $1 million in profits, less $230,000 (approximate) salaries for the husband/wife, yields a pre-tax distribution of $770,000. Saving 2.9% on that amount is a substantial $22,330. Both Ross and Sharon receive maximum Social Security benefits and they pay the minimum Medicare tax.

They must consider whether their salary is fair. It can be on the low end of the fair salary range, but it must be fair. Additionally, they must consider that provisional income in retirement may tax their future Social Security benefit.

In conclusion, tax planning and business ownership is as much about personal preference as it is about the math. Consider maximizing FICA for at least one spouse and consider doing so for both spouses. Even though this may cost you more in taxes today, you will potentially get more Social Security income later. Alternatively, you may want to minimize your taxable income today and not depend upon the government's Social Security, in which case you need to plan for yourself. Remember that the Medicare tax savings is the key advantage of a Subchapter S corporation tax election for companies with large profits. Companies with smaller profits could benefit from both Social Security tax savings and Medicare tax savings.

Solo 401k

A sole proprietor and his or her spouse can set up a solo 401k. If both spouses are employed by the business, then both of them may contribute to their 401k. Their contribution limits are much higher in a 401k than in an IRA, and the costs of a solo 401k are minimal. Many inexpensive investment custodians are available.

Additionally, a 401k plan enables the owners to put in employer contributions, which could more than double their deductible contributions. The 401k plan rules get complicated quickly, and this topic is discussed at greater length in the next chapter.

For Ross and Sharon, both over the age of 50, they can each contribute $23,000 into their solo 401k plan in 2013. They have until the end of the calendar year to make contributions. If they want to make employer contributions, they have until the date they file taxes to make these payments.

Taking Advantage of Business Losses

The business may pay you a salary but generate a loss on the tax return. You may be able to use the losses to offset taxes due on your salary received. You might be able to use these losses to offset the taxes due on a Roth conversion. This could help you move money out of the tax-deferred category and into the tax-free category. Business tax losses not used in this year carry forward and can be used in future years.

Tax Deductible Benefit Plans

Business owners can create tax-deductible benefit plans that give them more choice and control over their income. Many of these plans are discussed elsewhere in this book. Each of them has pros and cons, benefits, and costs. In almost every case, we pay for more choice and control with increased complexity. What works well for a neighbor or a friend is likely not appropriate for you. Finding balance is a key to success in all asset categories.

And Why Not?

Owning a business is not for everyone.

Are You Sure?

Owning your own business is a lot of work and is not for everyone. The freedom to work when you want and how much you want is sometimes too much for someone who may not be a self-starter and thus, may not get paid. Even if you do the work, there is no guarantee that your endeavor will lead to financial success.

Complications

Business ownership appeals to folks who do not mind taking on more risk and making things more complicated to have a little more control. As an employee, you might not get everything you want, but you are not solely responsible for the success of the entity. The business owner constantly balances finite time and resources with the demands of the marketplace, clients, suppliers, partners, and, of course, his or her own desires. And there is no assurance that the company will make money over the long-term or even be viable. Of course, the tax advantages discussed here assume that the company is profitable!

Go Tax Free in Executive Benefit Plans

CHAPTER 15

Absolute: Owners may be executives, but not all executives are owners.

Absolute: The older we are, the more serious our money questions become.

How This Benefits Me

For business owners, executive benefit plans accomplish many goals, including tucking away large amounts of money and having more choice and control over when and how they are taxed. Additionally, these plans can help retain and attract top talent, become part of the owner's exit plan, and ensure a tax-advantaged and successful business succession.

Example

Bonnie, in her sixties, is a rainmaker for a professional services firm. She recently left her prior employer to help this small firm grow and, with her reputation and connections, she is a real asset. To lure her talents away from her prior position, the owners of her new company give her a full suite of executive retirement benefits. She has a 401k, which she plans to maximize, and the company's profit-sharing plan, which depends upon the team's performance. However, the non-qualified Supplemental Executive Retirement Plan

(SERP) is the most appealing to Bonnie because it is different from anything she has seen before and it is customized for her. Here, she has a certain number of years to participate and a much larger retirement benefit than she could normally receive from another source. She's a motivated and enthusiastic top executive.

Corporate Plans at a Glance

Business owners and executives pay more in taxes than almost any other category of American; they also have more choice and control over these taxes than almost anyone else. Corporate benefit plans can be structured just for the executive or for the rank and file. Rank-and-file benefit plans have tax advantages that many folks may or may not be maximizing, so we will start with these plans. Then, we will look at executive benefit plans.

401k Planning

We discussed the benefits of a 401k plan in detail earlier. This is the starting place for deferring income taxes today in a traditional 401k and paying taxes now, and never again, in a Roth 401k. Since the 401k is qualified with the IRS, everyone in the organization must receive some equal level of benefit. Business owners and highly-compensated employees can structure their plans so that they can put away even more money than the current contribution maximums. The following summary will help you become familiar with 401k terminology so that you can ask the right questions.

Employee vs. Employer: Whose Money is It?

There are two ways to put money into a 401k: from the employee's deferred compensation and from the employer's contribution. In 401k terminology, the difference between employee and employer is very important, even for small companies. The employee contribution limits are outlined earlier in this book (see chapter four). These employee contribution limits are smaller in comparison to employer contributions.

Each of the following 401k planning ideas comes from the employer's wallet, not from the employee's contributions. If an owner wants to contribute more money into his 401k retirement plan, then he or she must contribute something into the employee's plans as well. All of the employer's contributions must be tax-deferred and cannot go into an after-tax Roth 401k.

Safe Harbor

Safe harbor plans give every employee a base level benefit and allow the highly compensated to contribute a greater amount of money in their 401k plans. One common safe harbor plan is the 3% non-elective safe harbor, which gives every employee 3%, regardless of whether the employee contributes to his or her own 401k. Another popular safe harbor plan is the safe harbor match. Here, an employer might match an employee's contributions 100% on the first 3% and then 50% on the next 2%. In this case, if an employee puts in 5%, the employer contributes 4%. Another popular option is a 100% match on the first 4%. Many variations exist. An owner may contribute more, but not less than one of these plans, on behalf of his or her employees and be in compliance with safe harbor provisions.

Acronyms

To prevent abuse, the IRS has developed a series of rules and regulations surrounding plans. The rules are designed to prevent abuse and ensure that plans benefit all employees and not just highly compensated employees. A safe harbor plan provides a comparatively simple set of rules, similar to a "get out of testing free" card, so that the plan may fail one of the following tests if they are a safe harbor plan. Briefly, owners should know the following language.

HCE *stands for highly compensated employee.* This refers to an owner, a direct family member of an owner (spouse, child, grandchild, parent, or grandparent), or anyone who makes more than $115,000 per year in 2013.[xxxvi]

ADP *tests are Actual Deferral Percentage tests.* Plans fail ADP tests for two reasons. Either an HCE contributes more than 2% more than non-HCE employees or the HCE contributes more than 125% of the average non-HCE employee's contributions.

ACP *tests are Annual Contribution Percentage tests.* ACP tests include the employer match and the employee after-tax contribution. Plans must pass both ACP and ADP tests or must be safe harbor plans in order to qualify with the IRS.

Profit Sharing

A key benefit of a 401k with profit-sharing plan is that the employer contribution limit on these plans is $51,000 per year per person in 2013.[xxxvii]

Profit-sharing plans are qualified plans, meaning some of the benefits must go to the rank-and-file employees as well as to the HCEs. These contributions are discretionary. In other words, the employer decides every year how much, if any, to put into the profit-sharing plan.

Defined Benefit Plan

A defined benefit (DB) plan enables much larger contributions than the 401k, closer to $200,000 per year per employee in 2013.[xxxviii] An older employer owner, or highly compensated employee, needs to tuck away much more for his or her retirement than a younger employee, and a defined benefit plan is one way to do it. Unlike a 401k, which is focused on the contributions, the DB plan focuses on retirement income. An actuary calculates how much income a participant needs, at what time, and makes assumptions about what rate of interest the plan will earn. Then, the present contribution is calculated.

Note: In today's low-interest rate world, higher contributions are allowed.

DB plans are qualified and benefits must go to all employees. The employer company assumes investment risk in order to provide the future income streams. Thus, DB plans, although they provide large deductible contributions, put risks on the employer.

Cash Balance Plan

A cash balance (CB) plan enables deductible contributions in the order of $200,000 per employee per year in 2013.[xxxix] A CB plan provides a lump sum at retirement. Popular with owners who expect much larger tax bills today than in the future, the CB plan is less risky for the employer than the DB plan. Although cash balance plans must also provide an income annuity option, the benefit is defined as a lump sum, which the employee is likely to take.

Executive Benefit Plans

Executive benefit plans are nonqualified, meaning they allow the executives to put away more money on a tax-advantaged basis than qualified plan limits allow.

Nonqualified plans are discriminatory. In other words, not everyone can participate in the plan or they risk becoming subject to the qualified plan limits. Nonqualified plans have no contribution or age limits. Instead, they are much more flexible.

Nonqualified Deferred Compensation Plan

The nonqualified deferred compensation (NQDC) plan enables companies to attract and keep top talent. Typically, these are salespeople and key executives, and it could be the owners. The employee may defer a large part of his or her compensation into the plan, avoiding income tax in that year. However, the company must pay income tax on the deferral. When the employee elects to receive the income, then the employer gets a deduction, just as if it were a salary.

This type of plan is an exciting way to retain top talent who wants to defer larger portions of otherwise taxable income.

Top Hat Plan

A top hat plan is a nonqualified deferred compensation plan for a small number of employees that enables much larger contributions than qualified plans. Top hat plans must follow the NQDC rules. Generally speaking, a top hat plan enables key executives to choose how much they want to defer. The employer does not fund a plan for them. Instead, the employer keeps the asset and liability on the balance sheet— which causes a tax burden to the employer in the year the employee makes the deferral. Then, upon the employee's exit, the entire top hat plan is taxable to the employee.

SERP: Supplemental Executive Retirement Plan

A supplemental executive retirement plan, or SERP, is a nonqualified plan where the contributions are made by the employer on behalf of a small number of key executives. They must follow the rules of nonqualified plans regarding non-funding and small numbers of key executives. SERP contributions are determined by the employer. They are discretionary. They usually involve a calculation of the executive's future income needs and sources, including Social Security and other pension benefits, and then the SERP funds the difference. They can be linked to performance of the individual, team, or company. They can be far more restrictive or liberal in scope than a qualified plan. Compared with qualified plans, employers can be more creative with vesting schedules and other rules that protect the employer. Assets are subject to the company's general creditors.

Unfunded and Select Employees Only

All of the nonqualified plans must remain unfunded. This is the opposite of a 401k or other qualified plan, which has separate assets allocated for the explicit use of the participants. A nonqualified plan cannot have the assets set aside, unless they are in a rabbi trust, discussed next.

A nonqualified plan must be for the benefit of a select number of employees only. The IRS assumes that certain employees who can negotiate their pay are more responsible than most employees, and do not need the protection of the qualified plans.

Rabbi Trust

An employer may set up a rabbi trust, with rules limiting the use of the assets, assuring participants that they will only be used for their benefit. However, rabbi trust assets are still subject to the general creditors of the company. Contrast this with a qualified plan where assets are separate from the company. In a 401k, the company could go bankrupt and participants would still have their money. This is not so in nonqualified plans.

Again, greater deferrals, greater flexibility, the ability to choose the timing of the tax payment, and the option to use life insurance, combine to make SERPs and other nonqualified plans appealing for a small number of executives.

Life Insurance

In a nonqualified deferred compensation plan, employers often offer an investment in life insurance. This way, all future growth is income-tax free. Plus, the employee's family and/or the company have death benefits. The company could receive a benefit if the insured dies. The employer benefits from not having to pay the income tax bill on the cash value growth of the policy.

When benefits and contributions are "split" between the employer and the employee, it is called split-dollar life insurance. Split-dollar is commonplace but not necessary. The flexibility of the plan structure and the unique features of the life insurance give the business owner and key employee several advantages. Cash values, and their tax advantages, and the vesting schedules and rules combine for a lot of creative solutions. Additionally, the policy can be structured in a way that the company can recover its costs if an employee dies. The employee's beneficiaries can receive a lump sum benefit upon his or her death.

And Why Not?

Executive benefit plans avoid some of the confusion associated with qualified plans, and come with some of their own complexities as well.

Non-Qualified is Not For Everyone

A small number of executives cannot mean everyone in the company. To keep the benefits safe from qualified plan rules, an expert must evaluate and structure the plan accordingly.

Life Insurance is Not The Answer to Every Problem

Life insurance is one of the most popular ways to fund nonqualified plans, but it is not the only way to fund it. Other vehicles include equities, with long-term capital gains on the sale and deferral of taxes while held. Tax benefits of stocks are also appealing. Life insurance requires underwriting, and the premium schedule, although flexible, is not "zero." It does require commitment from the employer.

General Creditors

Nonqualified plans, for participants, are always subject to the general creditors of the corporation. A rabbi trust puts rules around the assets set aside by the company to pay these benefits. If a company faces financial troubles, general creditors (not employees) have first claims on the assets whether they are in a rabbi trust or not.

Who is in Charge Here?

By creating a deferred compensation program where the executive non-business owner decides how much to defer, that same person is choosing (to some extent) the tax liability of the company. Remember, the nonqualified plans are nondeductible plans for the employer. When the employee retires, early or otherwise, then the employer receives the tax deduction. Until then, the employee defers taxation and the company pays the tax. Thus, a nonqualified plan in which the employer retains control of the taxation, like a SERP, is more appealing to the owner and less appealing to the executive non-owner.

Go Tax Free in Other Company Benefit Plans

Absolute: The simplest answer is often the best answer.

Absolute: Education makes the complex simple.

How This Benefits Me

Many services you are spending money on already may be tax deductible through a company plan, including life insurance, health insurance, general health expenses, education, parental care, childcare, etc. For business owners only, a Private Insurance Company is a new plan with significant, unique potential benefits.

Example

Inside Julio's company benefit plans, he has a host of options to help him go tax free. He chooses to defer as much as he can into the company's flexible spending account. He maximizes the company's life insurance option, especially the permanent plan. He takes advantage of the wellness plans and uses the extra pre-tax money exercising at the recreation center. Julio uses the educational funds to increase his technological skills at the local community college. He benefits not just from the tax savings but from being able to do more things, faster, and from the friendships he has formed at the school over the years. All told, Julio saves hundreds of dollars in taxes and feels more choice and control over his future.

Go Tax Free in Other Company Benefit Plans   195

Overview

Company benefit plans offer employees many options for going tax free, or at least deferring taxes. The plans each have pros and cons, limits and restrictions, and some or all of these may be a benefit for you and your situation.

Health Plans

Health insurance has been a part of corporate America since the 1940s when General Motors and other large companies needed ways to attract employees during the wage freezes of World War II. As you are well aware, in these plans the company makes insurance premium payments and the participant gets discounted healthcare. Lately, companies have shared with their employees the costs of the benefits, and employees are often surprised by how much money this adds up to be.

In the near future, plans that make the costs more visible to employees are likely to increase in popularity.

Health Savings Account

A health savings account (HSA) is owned by the individual and requires a high-deductible health insurance plan. Pre-tax dollars are contributed and spent on qualified medical expenses, including prescription medicine. The key advantage of the HSA over the flexible spending account, discussed below, is that if the money is not used in the plan year, the money rolls over into the future. The 2013 contribution limit for an HSA is $3,250 for an individual, $6,450 for a family and $1,000 additional catch-up contribution for age 50 years or older. [xl]

Flexible Spending Account

A flexible spending account (FSA) is a pre-tax savings vehicle similar to an HSA, set up through a company. It gives employees the ability to spend money on qualified medical expenses and, unlike the HSA, on dependent care also. The FSA is set up by the company, is not portable like the HSA, and you must "use it or lose it" during the plan year.

The medical FSA works with traditional health insurance plans and with high-deductible plans. The medical FSA is capped at $2,500 per year per employee.[xli] Many employers issue FSA credit cards to help employees comply with the "qualified" expense rules.

The dependent care FSA is a reimbursement plan capped at $5,000 per year.[xlii] You may spend this money on elderly parents or on your children's daycare, among other qualifying expenses. So, the FSA is both a little better than the HSA and more limiting than the HSA.

Group Life Insurance Plans

Companies often offer life insurance in their benefits package. Usually a group plan requires few, if any, underwriting requirements and pays a multiple of the employee's paycheck with options to buy more insurance. The purchased insurance is after tax so that the employee's family will receive the death benefit income-tax free.

Group Term Life Insurance

The most common and least expensive policy is a term life insurance policy. Upon the employee's exit, he or she may have the option to keep the policy. However, in most cases when an employee exits, the policy ceases. Thus, this is a very temporary solution.

Group Permanent Life Insurance

Companies can set up permanent group life insurance policies. This is less popular but in some cases more powerful than group term insurance. Group permanent policies accumulate money income-tax free and, upon the exit of an employee, the money sticks with the employee. Employees could accumulate money in excess of their 401k contributions and earn rates of return linked to a variable universal policy or a fixed universal policy. Earnings on these accounts benefit from the tax shelter of life insurance. Additionally, excess contributions are available prior to age 59½ without penalty.

Again, permanent life insurance is a cash accumulation vehicle with tax advantages, giving folks more choice and control over their income and their assets.

Employer Provided Education Assistance

Employers can write off $5,250 per year in education for their employees directly related to their job duties.[xliii] The credit counts toward tuition, books, and fees. Importantly, it does not include meals, lodging, or transportation. The education must have a reasonable relationship to your business. This plan is for everyone in the company and may not give more than 5% of its benefits to a highly compensated employee (HCE) in any given year.

Property and Casualty Insurance

Only applicable for owners of fairly large, steady cash-flow businesses, a complex new business tax planning strategy has become popular in recent years. The next few paragraphs provide a high-level understanding of this plan.

The Private Insurance Company (PIC) is a way for a profitable, established, and fairly good size privately-held business to address risks not covered in traditional property and casualty insurance plans. The business sets up a new company, 100% owned by the original company, and funds it with tax-deductible premiums.

The Private Insurance Company has its own expenses, books and tax records. The PIC must invest the premiums conservatively so that, in the event that one of the risks actually takes place, the PIC can cover the costs. The PIC needs to be funded with regular annual premiums, must hire an actuary and attorneys, and must meet the qualifications of an insurance company. Some PIC plan providers group unrelated businesses, which may or may not be a risk or provide benefits that are appropriate for you.

The advantages for the PIC owner exist upon exit. For a properly-run PIC business, the exit plan is the payment of a long-term capital gain (LTCG) tax on the value of the PIC. Each year, premiums, less expenses, less claims paid, increase the value of the PIC business. The dissolution of the PIC requires the owner to pay LTCG tax.

In other words, the business owner moved pre-income tax earnings into the PIC, ran the business and paid appropriate expenses, and then dissolved the PIC at long-term capital gains tax rates, saving a bundle on income taxes. You can see the appeal. The devils are in the details, and the experts you hire to run this business will largely determine your success.

And Why Not?

The company plans outlined here have pros and cons.

Specific Purpose Limits

The money in HSA, FSA and education plans generally can only be spent on a particular purpose. The medical FSA in particular has a "use it or lose it" provision that makes planning ahead critical. The HSA avoids that trap because it can accumulate money over time. In both cases, the money must be used on qualified medical expenses. The dependent care FSA is a reimbursement plan. If it is not used, the $5,000 tax deduction is lost.

Life Insurance Limits

Group permanent life insurance plans offer more flexibility in how and when the excess cash values can be used, but these are long-term plans. Life insurance takes a long time to accumulate significant cash values. As discussed in earlier chapters, the pros and cons are many.

Private Insurance Company, Are You Kidding?

The final plan in this chapter deals with property and casualty insurance, and is for owners of successful businesses only. It involves creating an entirely new insurance business. Does a business owner really want to be in the insurance business? What are the chances that one of these claims will be paid or that the IRS will change their tune and declare these plans are abusive tax shelters?

Only you can decide. If you are fortunate enough to be an owner with a large enough business to qualify for this plan, do your homework and plan for contingencies. Clearly, the advantages of turning income tax into long-term capital gains tax are appealing. Is all this work worth the effort?

CHAPTER 17

Go Deep

Absolute: In our end is our beginning.

We end as we began, with a story. What happens next is completely up to you. After you read this, I recommend you go back to that introductory chapter, print the questions, and start the search for your financial professional.

Example: Mountain Homes Utilities

Although I've changed the names, this is an example of one of our firm's favorite clients and how they took a few of these good ideas and put their experts to use in the best possible way for their unique situation.

Some years ago, Bill, Mitch, and Dave were police officers bemoaning their low-paying, high-stress jobs. Bill lived in the mountains, and Mitch and Dave, avid hunters and outdoorsmen, loved the mountains. They dreamed about living and working up there. They knew many mountain homes did not have natural gas. Instead, these homeowners had to pay a lot of money to have a truck come to their house and fill up a propane tank. And so the three men began talking about a business plan and started to move toward achieving their dreams.

To make a long story short, one summer Bill, Mitch, and Dave rented a backhoe and brought natural gas into Bill's neighborhood. All of Bill's neighbors signed up. The utility company paid the men for the service. The utility also paid them an ongoing premium for delivering the natural gas to these remote residents.

Then the utility company asked them to do it again. Mitch got the permits, Bill became the sales guy, and Dave took on operations. Before they knew it, they hired a handful of contract employees and had a real business going. They mortgaged their homes, quit the police department, and never looked back.

I met the Mountain Homes gang when they were staffing up. Together, along with their CPA, insurance experts, and an attorney, we helped them grow from six folks to several hundred employees and annual revenues measured not in millions, but in tens of millions of dollars.

From cops to capitalists, the success of these three dreamers epitomizes what happens when you lean on experts and focus on where you are going, not just where you are.

One of the first things we did was dump the Simple IRA and start a 401k. With only a handful of folks, a 401k looked like overkill for the situation at the time. However, we had the foresight to implement a plan that was perfect for the company they intended to become. And they did grow!

Today, the Mountain Homes gang faces a situation where the three founders have had all the success they envisioned. They want to leave a legacy for their families. Additionally, Bill's son now runs much of the operations and is the heir apparent. So, we are working on the executive plans discussed in this book to help them achieve a very different set of goals:

1. Enabling the heir apparent to run the business.
2. Motivating and retaining non-owner executives.
3. Providing for contingencies.
4. Reducing taxes!

One advisor, like your author, could not do this alone. Clearly, this is an example of what happens when a successful business owner has assembled a team of professionals. Additionally, this is an example of going deep.

Go Deep

You do not need to implement many of these plans to achieve your goals. You certainly should not attempt to implement all of them. Instead of casting a wide net and being confused and indecisive about so many changing plans and tax rules, go deep.

Focus on your goals and your core values. Implement plans that align with who you want to become or what your company is becoming. Don't limit yourself to who you are today. Instead, focus on who you intend to become.

The Mountain Home gang built a business that most of us would love to have. They are larger than many companies and they started with no more than a dream. They have already achieved more financial success than their founders imagined. The next generation of executives is in a good place to take the company to an even higher level. They have a complex business with a lot of moving parts, regulations, and people to track. One of their desires, however, is simple:

We want to grow and protect our investments, and we want more choice and control over taxes.

To help them achieve these goals, an expert team went deep with a couple of plans. We did not implement everything. In fact, we had to unwind the short-sighted Simple plan which limited their growth. Instead, we built and are building for the company they are becoming.

Perhaps the Most Important Story I've Ever Heard or Told

At the beginning of this book, I promised to end where I began. So here is my gift to you. Find a quiet place and turn on your imagination.

In a few short minutes, you will finish this book and walk outside. You have to cross a street. Imagine that street corner. Imagine the most dangerous street corner in your neighborhood. Now, imagine that you are alone waiting to cross the most dangerous street you know. What is the first thing you do?

Look both ways. That's right! You assess the risks before you begin the journey. And you are nervous.

The lights turn red. Traffic comes to a stop. Your heart races. This road is dangerous, but now is your time to move. Just as you step off the curb, you feel a brush at your elbow and you are shocked. You thought you were alone, but you're not. Someone is beside you. Who is it? You look down at your elbow and what do you see?

An elderly person, waiting to cross the road, stands beside you. A minute ago you were worried about how you are going to cross the road. Can you imagine what she must be feeling? She must be thirty years older than you are. How is she going to make it? In fact, you feel that she will not make it without your help. So what do you do?

You help her. Of course you do! You reach out your arm, and she looks up at you. She doesn't say a word, but she smiles. And you feel good.

You set off at your regular pace across the road. You make it two steps and you've already left her behind. Now what? You take a step back, gently hold her elbow, and you proceed at her pace, not yours. Are you with me? You shuffle. And you shuffle. And you shuffle. One lane of traffic. And you shuffle. Now you are in the second lane of traffic. And you shuffle. And then what happens?

The light changes. Now what do you do? Do you run away? Grab her and throw her over your shoulder? Of course not! You likely do something like the Heisman Trophy pose and say, in your own way, "Stop traffic!"

This is the moment you are living for. This is the question we will all answer, in one way or another, before we die. Why is it that you are out in the middle of this most dangerous intersection, risking your life for someone you don't know and may never see again? How did you get here? Why do you stay?

The answers are profound. They reveal, at least in part, why no matter what the world's economies will throw our way, regardless of whatever terrorist or other threat we may ever face, we will survive because we always stick together when we need to most. Can you feel that? Don't you know that to be true?

You look at your companion and say: "We better get a move on!"

When her eyes meet yours, you have an epiphany. This is the moment you've been waiting for. We will all have this moment at some point in our lives. You have never seen her before. Her body is smaller, weaker, and slower than yours, both mentally and physically. But when her eyes meet your eyes, you see your own eyes looking back, thirty years from now.

The person you are becoming is with you today. She is completely dependent upon the decisions you make today. And every decision you defer only increases the burden on the person you are becoming.

It's our great gift to be guides. It is our blessing to walk the most dangerous roads of our clients' lives together and to hold back the traffic that may, without us, ruin them. Someday, I too will grow weary and perhaps incapable of managing my own wealth. I too will need a guide.

I encourage you to find your guide. Make them know you, your goals, your values, and your whole person. Then hold them accountable. And make that decision sooner, rather than later.

It's been my blessing to be your guide in these pages. God bless.

Appendix A: Employed or Unemployed?

Some plans are best for people who are employed. Other plans work whether you are employed or unemployed.

	Employed	Not Employed
IRA	YES	NO
Roth IRA	YES	NO
Roth Conversion	YES	YES
Roth 401k	YES	NO
OUR Plan	YES	YES
Annuity	YES	YES
Arbitrage Annuity and Life	YES	YES
Charitable Trust	YES	YES

	Employed	Not Employed
Lifetime Trusts	YES	YES
Education Savings Plans	YES	YES
Municipal Bonds	YES	YES
Stocks	YES	YES
Real Estate	YES	YES
Own Business	YES	NO
Executive Benefit Plans	YES	NO
Company Benefit Plans	YES	NO

Appendix B: Safety or Growth?

Some investors are more interested in preserving their invested dollars. Others are more interested in growth potential.

	Potential Safety	Growth Potential
IRA	YES	YES
Roth IRA	YES	YES
Roth Conversion	YES	YES
Roth 401k	YES	YES
OUR Plan	YES	YES
Annuity	YES	YES
Arbitrage Annuity and Life	YES	NO
Charitable Trust	YES	YES

	Potential Safety	Growth Potential
Lifetime Trusts	YES	YES
Education Savings Plans	NO	NO
Municipal Bonds	YES	NO
Stocks	NO	YES
Real Estate	YES	YES
Own Business	NO	YES
Executive Benefit Plans	YES	YES
Company Benefit Plans	YES	NO

Appendix C: Long or Short Time Horizon?

Some strategies are best for long-term planning and others work best in the short term. Almost always, a plan that is best in the short term pays a price over the long-term. Due to inflation, some strategies may not deliver the same purchasing power in the future.

	Long-Term Time Horizon	Short-Term Time Horizon
IRA	YES	NO
Roth IRA	YES	NO
Roth Conversion	YES	NO
Roth 401k	YES	NO
OUR Plan	YES	NO
Annuity	YES	Immediate Annuity
Arbitrage Annuity and Life	YES	YES

	Long–Term Time Horizon	Short–Term Time Horizon
Charitable Trust	YES	Maybe
Lifetime Trusts	YES	NO
Education Savings Plans	YES	YES
Municipal Bonds	NO	YES
Stocks	YES	NO
Real Estate	MAYBE	MAYBE
Own Business	YES	YES
Executive Benefit Plans	YES	NO
Company Benefit Plans	YES	YES

List of References

[i] Tax Foundation website, May 3, 2012, Kevin Duncan. http://taxfoundation.org/article/americans-paying-more-taxes-food-clothing-and-shelter

[ii] 2013 estimated budget deficit, as of January 2013, is one trillion dollars. http://en.wikipedia.org/wiki/2013_United_States_federal_budget. The 2012 budget deficit was worse, $1.327 trillion. http://en.wikipedia.org/wiki/2012_United_States_federal_budget

[iii] These questions come from, in part, the Financial Planning Association, a good place to start a search for a Financial Planning Professional: www.fpanet.org

[iv] http://www.taxpolicycenter.org/taxtopics/2013-Allow-top-two-rates-to-rise.cfm

[v] The IRS provides a state income tax deduction which slightly reduces the total taxes owed. In this example, it is not as simple as adding 4.63% state plus 10% federal.

[vi] online.wsj.com/article/SB10001424127887323820104578216092043022764.html [1/1/13] Additionally, in 2013 the Unearned Income Medicare Contribution Tax imposes 3.8% additional tax on Net Investment Income or Modified Adjusted Gross Income above the following thresholds:

- $250,000 for married filing joint filers and qualifying widows or widowers;
- $200,000 for single and head of household filers; and
- $125,000 for married filing separately filers.

[vii] Publication 915, Social Security and Equivalent Railroad Retirement Benefits

[viii] Publication 590, Individual Retirement Arrangements (IRAs)

[ix] Publication 590, Individual Retirement Arrangements (IRAs)

[x] Publication 590, Individual Retirement Arrangements (IRAs)

[xi] Publication 590, Individual Retirement Arrangements (IRAs)

[xii] Assumes a 8% rate of return for 30 years.

[xiii] www.bls.gov

[xiv] The cost doubles every ten years because it assumes an approximate 7% interest rate. However, it could easily have doubled every nine years with an 8% inflation rate, which is about the rate of increase in healthcare costs.

[xv] IRS Publication 575 Pension and Annuity Income. See also clarifications from the IRS 401(k) Resource Guide, found here: http://www.irs.gov/Retirement-Plans/Plan-Sponsor/401(k)-Resource-Guide---Plan-Sponsors---General-Distribution-Rules (d. 2/5/2013)

[xvi] Burns, Scott, "Most Need More Life Insurance," Dallas Morning News, October 6, 2004.

[xvii] Burns, Scott, "Most Need More Life Insurance," Dallas Morning News, October 6, 2004.

[xviii] Certain types of term insurance called "Return of Premium" (ROP) insurance are a noteworthy exception to this rule. ROP insurance is not permanent.

[vxix] Fixed whole life policies can offer guaranteed premium payments, but a variable whole life could see its investment accounts lose value, requiring the owner to pay more money into the account to keep the same death benefit.

[xx] Variable universal life is sold by prospectus. Please consider the investment objectives, risks, charges, and expenses before investing. The prospectus, which contains this and other information about the variable universal life insurance policy and the underlying investment options, can be obtained from your financial professional. Be sure to read the prospectus carefully before deciding whether to invest.

[xxi] Assumes the contract qualifies as life insurance under section 7702 of the Internal Revenue Code (IRC) and is not a Modified Endowment Contract (MEC) under section 7702A. Most distributions are taxed on a First In First Out (FIFO) basis as long as the contract meets non-MEC definitions under section 7702A. Loans and partial withdrawals from a MEC will generally be taxable and, if taken prior to age 59 ½, may be subject to a 10% penalty.

[xxii] The estate tax schedule is subject to change and available on our web site, www.assetsandincome.com.

[xxiii] Variable annuities are long-term investment vehicles designed for retirement purposes. They are sold by prospectus. Please consider the investment objectives, risks, charges, and expenses carefully before investing. The prospectus, which contains this and other information about the variable annuity contract and the underlying investment options, can be obtained from your financial professional. Be sure to read the prospectus carefully before deciding whether to invest.

[xxiv] IRS Publication 970 Qualified Tuition Plan.

[xxv] Barrons Finance and Investment Handbook, Eighth Edition, pub. October 1, 2010, Barrons Educational Series, Inc. http://stockcharts.com/freecharts/historical/spxusb1978.html

[xxvi] Mutual funds are sold by prospectus. Please consider the investment objectives, risks, charges, and expenses carefully before investing. The prospectus, which contains this and other information about the investment company, can be obtained from your financial professional. Be sure to read the prospectus carefully before deciding whether to invest.

[xxvii] In January 2013, the ten-year treasury yield was more than 1.5% and less than 1.9%. The S&P 500 Dividend Yield was over 2.6% and under 3%. For a current yield curve and history, visit www.stockcharts.com. For the current S&P 500 dividend yield and history, visit: http://www.multpl.com/s-p-500-dividend-yield/

[xxviii] Barron's Finance and Investment Handbook, 3rd Edition, 2012.

[xxix] Barron's Finance and Investment Handbook, 3rd Edition, 2012.

[xxx] Inflation: BLM.gov

xxxi For an in-depth look at this phenomenon, called loss aversion, see Daniel Kahneman's discussion in his book Thinking, Fast and Slow, Fahrer, Straus and Giroux, 2011.

xxxii IRS Publication 523: Selling Your Home

xxxiii IRS Publication 936: Mortgage Interest Deduction, "qualified loan limit"

xxxiv IRS Publication 544: Sales and Other Dispositions of Assets, "depreciation recapture"

xxxv OASDI and SSI Program Rates and Limits 2013: http://www.ssa.gov/policy/docs/quickfacts/prog_highlights/index.html

xxxvi IRS Publication 560: Retirement Plans for Small Businesses

xxxvii IRS Publication 560: Retirement Plans for Small Businesses

xxxviii IRS Publication 560: Retirement Plans for Small Businesses (Defined Benefit) and http://www.irs.gov/Retirement-Plans/Plan-Participant,-Employee/Retirement-Topics---Defined-Benefit-Plan-Contribution-Limits

xxxix IRS Publication 560: Retirement Plans for Small Businesses (Cash Balance) and http://www.irs.gov/pub/irs-tege/epchd1104.pdf

xl IRS Publication 969: Health Savings Accounts and Other Tax-Favored Health Plans

xli IRS Publication 969: Health Savings Accounts and Other Tax-Favored Health Plans

xlii IRS Publication 969: Health Savings Accounts and Other Tax-Favored Health Plans

xliii Education benefits fall under IRC 127 and Section 132(d) Working Condition Benefit.

About the Author

Karl Frank owns A & I Financial Services LLC, a wealth management firm headquartered in Englewood, Colorado. The firm helps successful families and businesses grow and protect their wealth and choose how they want to be taxed.

Karl Frank is a leader in the Denver business and financial planning communities. He serves on the Board of Directors for the Financial Planning Association (FPA) of Colorado, where he helped found Denver Financial Planning Day. Karl is also a member of the Million Dollar Roundtable, with Top of the Table distinction. Karl enjoys public speaking and is a contributor to numerous publications.

In addition to his Certified Financial Planner® designation, Karl holds three Masters Degrees. He earned a Masters of Business Administration and Masters of Science in Finance from the University of Denver, Daniels College and Reimann School of Finance. He also has a Master of Arts in English from the University of Colorado at Boulder. He holds FINRA securities licenses 7, 24, 52, 63, 65, as well as his life insurance license.

Karl loves mountain sports, especially hiking and skiing. He also enjoys golfing, writing, and woodworking. Karl and his family live in Centennial, Colorado.

Visit www.assetsandincome.com to subscribe to Karl's weekly investment newsletter, view our video library, schedule Karl as a speaker, and access helpful resources.

Securities provided through Geneos Wealth Management Inc., member FINRA, SIPC. Investment advisory services offered through A & I Financial Services LLC, registered investment advisor.